WOMEN

Love, Drama, Support, Romance, Adventure, Family, Choices,
Emotions... so much knowledge

A book on all you need to know about women: The truth, myths and
secrets, through the lens of over 60 women in the bible.

JANELLE OBIEROMA

UnVeilinGrace TC Publishing
Email: unveilingracecounselling@gmail.com

Dedication

I dedicate this book to GOD ALMIGHTY, my heavenly Father. WOMEN OF LIFE is a reality only through the Grace of God and the power of the Holy Spirit. My heart is full of praise! Thank you, dear Lord Jesus, for everything.

To all the women who love to love and be loved, women who believe in kindness. Women who fight injustice, women who make things happen, women who get inspired rather than become envious or feel threatened by the successes of other women, women who support each other, women who fear God and trust in GOD. Cheers to us.

And, to all the men who care about the women in their lives; men, who cheer the sheer strength of women, understand the gender differences and give vigorous support to women everywhere.

This is for you and Ojiugo.

 Ojiugo

Ojiugo, also called Ojiuo, is my mother. She taught me a lot of great things. I took some of those things for granted because I felt they were general knowledge until I grew older, then I realised they were not common. We live in a world where unkindness is being normalised, where virtue is going extinct and shamelessness is being celebrated.

The other day we were talking on the phone when I told her I was going to write about her in my new book. She laughed and said, "No, I don't want attention". But I got her approval after telling her it was for a good cause. There are two kinds of people; the ones that were never taught to be kind, generous, virtuous, empathetic, prudent and God-fearing, and the ones who were taught but never accepted the training. For the sake of the former category, we need to talk about kindness more.

Ojiugo perfectly combines resilience and malleability. She can be strong-willed and yet so gentle and humble. She is very patient; I wonder how she does it because being tolerant doesn't come that naturally to me. She is a survivor; a testament to the grace and power of God. She is a staunch friend; someone you can share your deep concerns with because of her wisdom, amiable nature, child-like enthusiasm and God-fearing attribute. She can be quite a drama queen. I remember the first time I went on a date; my phone battery ran down from her incessant calls and I was delayed because I got caught in traffic. By the time I got home, I met her crying up a storm because my dad didn't know I went out and she was so afraid he would notice. To say it mildly, if daddy had noticed I wasn't home, it would not have been funny at all! That she wasn't able to reach me increased her anxiety. She probably thought I had eloped or been abducted by the young man.

Ojio is a natural philanthropist who loves to share what she has with others. She would say, "Gozie, carry the big bucket". "Why? To where?", I would ask. "I want you to put some yams and rice in a bag, put it inside the bucket, then put a wrapper on it and act like you want to fetch water. Then follow her downstairs and give her."

"Let me just give it to her straight away." "No, there are people in the sitting room. Just do it discreetly, as I said". She would insist.

I celebrate her grace; whenever we agreed she should not loan money to someone because the person refused to pay previous loans, she would still go ahead... her empathy leaves me in awe now but then I used to think it was foolish. I wonder how even though she never borrowed, she could understand the hardships people go through. She said to me, "Gozie, forget her former behaviour, allow me to lend to her ... it is not easy to beg, so, when someone begs and you have it, always give. God sees everything".

She let nothing stop her from being a blessing. We used to grumble... And try to negotiate our way out of those errands. My siblings and I didn't understand or encourage her... but as we grew older, we complained less because we began to notice the sheer joy on the faces of the beneficiaries. While we used to think about the discomfort; the stress of being the errand girls, carrying foodstuffs and clothes to different families. Mummy was busy thinking up unique plans just to share what she has with others. I remember the strategy of using rope and bucket to move foodstuffs downstairs from the kitchen balcony whenever Ationu was sitting at the dining table. Sometimes my mum would even bribe us just to send help to people. Several times she would force us... "Mummy, I cannot go to these places". I would grumble. "Isi gini? What did you say? Isi gbu onwe gi... Iye jelili". She will reply. On and on, we would murmur, "These bags are too heavy. What if I met my dad on the way? Where would I say I was going with all these things? This kind of mother Theresa's ministry is getting too much."

I celebrate your ingenuity. I remember how you used to secretly open bank accounts, because at that time, dad didn't think a woman should have an account. I remember how you used to panic and close them in order to avoid talebearing anytime you saw any of Dad's friends in the vicinity. Instead of staying without a saving, you calculated the risks and did this several times. As a future-forward female living in a patriarchal environment, you learned how to get what you want without unnecessary fights.

Today, I pray to be as selfless as you; the way you can hear God tell you to bless families and individuals is a strength I have realised is not common at all. I wish I could be as accommodating as you. I love the way you forgive and believe in the best of people. I never saw you fighting anyone, and whenever anyone fought you, you always trust God to defend you. I remember that day in Obosi after dad passed on when the argument about properties arose. You were crying, unable to exchange toxic words with that woman. Then one of my aunts walked into your room and said, "Is she not your fellow woman?" Why should you cry because of her lies? Stand up and tell her the story of her life. People may not stop oppressing you if they think you are afraid. I know you are not afraid, you just want peace... But remember, your husband is not here anymore. See, your children are looking at you." Then you went back into that sitting room and spoke in a way that made us glad. Your strong faith in God, your open-mindedness, your gentle toughness... Truly, your outward beauty is just an expression of your beautiful spirit. I celebrate a paragon of virtue, the quintessential mother. A perfect role model, my beautiful mother. God bless you abundantly always and continually use you for His glory in Jesus Christ's mighty name. I love and appreciate you, ma.

Chapters

Acknowledgement

I am eternally grateful to GOD for HIS loving-kindness. Thank you, Abba-Father, for the privilege of serving you. Thank you, dear Lord Jesus Christ, all the glory belongs to You. I am blessed to have the guidance of the Holy Spirit throughout this project and always.

I want to say a big thank you to the man that sweetens my heart, my darling husband. When I met you, my revelation about God's love deepened. It is a privilege to be your wife. You show me every day that love is kind, marriage is beautiful and strength is gentle. Thank you, sweetie, for loving me so completely.

The all-knowing God I serve saw this book before I was born and chose the perfect role model for me; my mother is the quintessential virtuous woman, loving beyond reason, resilient yet vulnerable, generous and wise, patient and tough.

I have the best sisters. I say this with all humility. Thanks a lot, girls, for your love and support. With a family like mine, I am doubly inspired to help more people experience and enjoy the bliss of genuine friendship, support and love that is found when we understand who a woman is. And the similarities and uniqueness among women.

Thank you to everyone who has been a blessing to me. You are too many to mention your names; my amazing family, leaders, pastors, clients, colleagues, brethren, mentees, staff and friends. I love and appreciate every one of you.

A big thank you to my amazing children for your wholehearted support and inspiring friendship.

Epigraph

My Father's Daughters

(Gender inequality)

"It's a girl!"

"Wow. Thank God, that's amazing... very beautiful. We will name her "Ifeoma" (meaning, good thing).

"It's a girl"

"Great, thank God for the safe delivery. We will name her "Chineze" (meaning; God protects)"

"It's a girl"

"Lovely, we will name her "Chigozie" (meaning, God bless).

"It is a girl..."

"Not again, okay, but I thought it would be a boy this time... nevertheless, God's time is the best. So, we will name her Ogechukwu (Meaning God's time)... because Ogechineke kanma... yes, God's time is the best."

... "It's a girl"

"That's beautiful. God has been with me, blessing and prospering me so I can take of these delightful children He has given me. We will call her Obiageli. She came to enjoy."

"It's a girl".
"Not again".

Is this a test or what? My friends are laughing at me. Everyone is talking behind my back. You are the mother; you name her whatever you want since you have embarrassed me like this. She was born on Sunday after all, so which other name should she bear? (Girls born on Sundays are usually called Ukamaka). What have I done to deserve this? Can't you have a male child? I think I should get another wife who would give birth to sons for me." She is as bright and beautiful as a fluorescent lamp. So, she was named Adaeze. Meaning: Princess.

"It is a girl".

Noooo, I refuse to deal with this anymore... this can't be happening again. Who did I offend to deserve this? You, this woman... do you know people are saying I have used my male seeds for money rituals and that's why I don't have male children? And yet you are still giving me girls... I don't have enough words to say to you. Don't you dare talk to me about her name? I don't care."

At that point, I think he could have shed tears. Daddy was beyond angry. Daddy was a good man, a protector and a provider.

But I think he let society condition him. He gave heed to their ignorant ridicule. This made him defensive about his blessings. Mummy later gave birth to two handsome sons, and my dad saw that sex did not determine the worth of a child. He loved everyone equally.

Mummy named the seventh girl Onyekachukwu (meaning; who is greater than God?). After considering naming her "Divine", because she was so pleasant, friendly, lively and beloved. Mummy loves her girls and will let no one tell her they are lesser than boys. Sometimes she felt hurt by the ignorance, myopia, and insensitivity of some people, but she let no one steal her joy.

My mom went through a lot, just for giving birth to girls. There were whispers and impertinent words uttered, mostly by her fellow women. My dad was made to feel like a fool for training his girls through college, especially at a private university! To avoid further ridicule, he ignorantly passed up several opportunities to invest because he felt he had no sons who would inherit his properties.

Mummy is the real MVP. She believes in the value of a girl-child. Seven beautiful girls! Everyone has a college degree; some have multiple degrees. Several are happily married with children. Indeed, God is gracious and kind.

As a woman with six sisters and many friends, I know what being a woman means in our society; the limitations society tries to place on our path and the battles we face and win squarely.

As one of my father's daughters, I have experiential knowledge about the misinformation and injustice that lack of parity between the sexes can cause. There are young girls in parts of the world who are working as servants because their families do not endorse or support the education of female children. Growing up then, sometimes people stared at us incredulously, not just because we were 7 pretty girls wearing similar pretty dresses but because we were girls whose parents provided for us. I had a sheltered childhood. I lacked nothing except the freedom to go anywhere I pleased. My dad was overly strict. I think he used to have a panic attack at the thought of one of his girls getting pregnant outside wedlock.

Fact remains that a girl-child is not inferior to a boy-child. They are different because of sexual organs, but where it matters most, they are the same. Gender does not play any role in our intellectual capacity, empathetic reasoning, leadership prowess, or interests.

Opportunities should not be made available only to the male. Several times, newly married women are ignored during recruitment processes. Once they say they do not have children yet, the recruiter does a mental calculation and figures they may soon need maternity leave. Imagine that, why should our value-adding, natural ability to birth and raise children be used as a disadvantage? Such unfair treatment is sending a subtle message: telling women to better not work. The decision to apply for a job is strictly the individual's, not society's. Some organisations pay women less than they would their male counterparts doing the same work.

Several societies create a glass ceiling against women, but the tensile strength of the glass ceiling varies from region to region. Gender inequality is rife in Africa. Hence, there is a need for massive sensitisation.

JANELLE OBIEROMA

Introduction

"Women of Life" is a compendium of the inspirational and dramatic lives of over 60 women in the Bible. This book gives us a deep insight into the 'WOMAN' God created, what you need to know about her, how to harness the power embedded in her and enjoy the blessings of being her, knowing her and loving her.

Knowledge exposes purpose; discovering purpose is the first requirement in determining value. When we understand the true purpose of a woman, then we can understand the value of a woman.

Women are powerful forces of influence. Whether for good or evil, no matter the roles they play- as mothers, wives, daughters, sisters, friends or staff. Their intuitive nature, strength, multitasking prowess and ability to nurture always make them a force to reckon with.

Everyone who wants to live a peaceful life must learn to give every woman in their life her rightful place and let her function in her unique role. This is so important because the average woman is multifaceted, far-reaching and boundless. Virtually every woman extends her relevance, infringes on other roles and grabs more territories, seriously, this is why we see mothers wanting to play the role of wives, wives wanting to take the place of mothers-in-law, sisters, female friends or even staff colliding into each other's role.

Wherever you see strife, heartbreak and marital issues, the core reason is not always far from this. Most women can endure anything but the snatching away of their roles, positions and rewards to give to another.

Many people bemoan the fact that women cannot be understood. I saw a funny meme encouraging men to give up on ever understanding women, it said: "if women shave off their God-given brows and draw another for themselves... if women exchange their natural breast for silicon... how can any man ever hope to understand or satisfy them?"

Are women that mysterious? Are women unpredictable?

After reading this book, you will not say you don't understand women ever again because we will glean from the surest knowledge, which is revealed by God, the creator of everything.

"Women of Life" was born 5 years ago as "Women of the Word" while I was praying with my husband. It started as a yearly conference I organise during the Mother's Day\ International Women's Day period. I tagged the first edition as "Women in the Word". Over the years, testimonies have been mind-blowing. Last year, 2020, we couldn't hold a physical conference because of the lock-down, so we had a virtual one. The inspiration to publish the book came when I was preparing for the online meetings.

As I prayed towards the conference, the Holy Spirit instructed me to study more intensively, compile my notes over the years and publish them; it will serve as a guide to everyone in understanding women. Over the years, the depth of knowledge in the Holy Bible has fascinated me... everything we need to know is in there; the uniqueness, drama, complexities, purpose and essence of women.

"For whatever things were written before were written for our learning, that we through the patience and comfort of the Scriptures might have hope. " Rom 15:4

"All scripture is given by inspiration of God, and is profitable for doctrine, for reproof, for correction, for instruction in righteousness:" 2 Tim 3:16 KJV

It's a great pleasure to write this book, and I am grateful to God for the privilege. I am super excited about "WOMEN OF LIFE". I would have loved to add a dancing emoji here, but let us look at the biblical accounts of several women and take some lessons from them. Then you will see why I wanted to add a dancing emoji. There is so much to learn and experience as we study these women's lives.

"And the Lord God said, "It is not good that man should be alone; I will make him a helper comparable to him."

...So Adam gave names to all cattle, to the birds of the air, and to every beast of the field. But for Adam, there was not found a helper comparable to him. And the Lord God caused a deep sleep to fall on Adam, and he slept, and He took one of his ribs and closed up the flesh in its place. Then the rib which the Lord God had taken from man He made into a woman, and He brought her to the man. And Adam said: "This is now bone of my bones And flesh of my flesh; She shall be called <u>Woman</u> Because she was taken out of Man."

Therefore, a man shall leave his father and mother and be joined to his wife, and they shall become one flesh. And they were both naked, the man and his wife, and were not ashamed." Gen 2:17-25

God made the woman to complete and complement man; woman was made as a helpmeet, a worthy fit... not inferior or lacking in grace or power. Women have always been influential; where women go, the nation goes. But after being deceived by the serpent, the woman misused her power and so God put a clip on it.

"Then the man said, "The woman whom You gave to be with me, she gave me of the tree, and I ate." And the Lord God said to the woman, "What is this you have done?" The woman said, "The serpent deceived me, and I ate." Gen 3:12-13

"To the woman, He said: "I will greatly multiply your sorrow and your conception; In pain, you shall bring forth children; Your desire shall be for your husband, And he shall rule over you." Gen 3:16

The above-underlined scripture shows how the woman became subject to man. It also shows us that woman, being subject to man, was not the initial plan; her subservient position resulted from a fall from grace caused by disobedience to God.

God wants and demands obedience from us. Being redeemed by the blood of Jesus and saved by Grace does not change this. Rather, grace allows us to be righteous despite the past and to have a right standing with God.

A gracious woman retains honour,
But ruthless men retain riches. Prov 11:16

What women love!

True feminism is an advocacy for women to freely express themselves:

- Women love to love and be loved.
- Women love to be cared for and to care.
- Women love to be understood and to understand.
- Women love to have, so they won't be at the mercy of others.
- Women love to be protected and to protect others.
- Women love to be given their place.
- Women love to be guided and also allowed to guide.
- Women love to be pampered and to work.
- Women love to be strong and to be fragile.
- Women love to receive attention and to give attention.
- Women love to respect and be treated with respect.
- Women love to be given and to give.

Their upbringing, environment and education usually influence most women, like most men. So, while the above list is a powerful guide on what an average woman wants, it is not necessarily what every woman wants.

Women are reciprocal beings; mostly, they give back what you give to them, literarily. With most women, whatever you sow is what you will reap. This knowledge is an expose that arms anyone who wants to develop a good relationship with a woman.

The default programming of a woman is to be highly reciprocal and naturally influential, with a high tendency to multiply her abilities. This makes it imperative for women to be properly educated and rightly motivated; a lot depends on women. It will be foolhardy to ignore women or not pay enough attention to their spiritual, intellectual and physical development.

The wise woman builds her house, but the foolish pulls it down with her hands. Prov 14:1

Some women out of deep love have turned seeds of hatred and inferiority into harvests of love and strength; such women yielded good fruits despite the evil seeds sown into them. Some women, out of greed and depravity, still bear rotten fruits despite the good done to them by others.

Virgin Mary

Virgin Mary is the woman who birthed our Lord Jesus. She was the wife of Joseph and cousin of Elizabeth. *"In the sixth month of Elizabeth's pregnancy, God sent the angel Gabriel to the Galilean village of Nazareth to a virgin engaged to be married to a man descended from David. His name was Joseph, and the virgin's name, Mary. Upon entering, Gabriel greeted her:*

> *Good morning!*
> *You're beautiful with God's beauty,*
> *Beautiful inside and out!*
> *God be with you.*

She was thoroughly shaken, wondering what was behind a greeting like that. But the angel assured her, "Mary, you have nothing to fear. God has a surprise for you: You will become pregnant and give birth to a son and call his name Jesus.

He will be great, be called 'Son of the Highest.' The Lord God will give him the throne of his father David; He will rule Jacob's house forever — no end, ever, to his kingdom."

Mary said to the angel, "But how? I've never slept with a man." The angel answered,

The Holy Spirit will come upon you, the power of the Highest hover over you; Therefore, the child you bring to birth will be called Holy, Son of God.

"And did you know that your cousin Elizabeth conceived a son, old as she is? Everyone called her barren, and here she is six months pregnant! Nothing, you see, is impossible with God."

And Mary said, Yes, I see it all now: I'm the Lord's maid, ready to serve. Let it be with me just as you say. Then the angel left her. Luke 1:26-38 MSB

Mary's faith is astounding; it takes a certain kind of faith to receive and believe such a unique assignment. I call it great faith. It takes great faith to accept what Angel Gabriel told her; the virgin birth is an unprecedented mind-blowing occurrence. It takes great faith to birth a miracle. Have you ever wondered how Mary felt when she was told her child will be called the son of the highest? Or that she would conceive without sleeping with a man?

There is nothing God has told you that is as awe-inspiring and enormous as what was told Mary. Yet Mary said, "Lord, let it be unto me according to thy Word!" So, take a cue from Mary and choose to believe what God has told you. Live a purposeful life to the glory of God, without fear or doubt.

Can your mind accept the blessings God has in store for you? Can it grasp eternity? Can you accept the power of divinity? Can you conceive of a miracle? Can you take a leap of faith? Can you move even when you cannot fathom the way? Can you choose to ignore the 'how' question and rather say, "Yes Lord, here I am, use me?" Can you believe God's word, as big and impossible as it may appear?

What has God told you about your life? What has He said about your prosperity? He has said the path of the just shall shine brighter and brighter. He has said He would prosper the work of your hands... Believe and Reaffirm His Words! What has He said about your marriage, health, and finances?

Last year I held a ticketed event for couples. During the couple segment (which I was not supposed to handle by the way, but by what I later got to know was divine orchestration, the lady who we expected to handle it had to leave before that segment of the event began).

After asking a wife to say her husband's top three favourite countries... I asked a certain husband a question: "What would your wife pay anything for... if she had a million dollars, what would she spend in it on?"

"She will want her own child; she loves jewellery too". He whispered. We continued with the program; having fun and learning new stuff.

At the close of the event, I asked them to wait. Then I called my husband, who is also a pastor, aside. (He had attended the program as the guest minister who handled the renewal of vows segment). I pleaded with him to pray with the couple because I perceived they required a miracle. He didn't plan to minister to anyone, especially on that day, but he agreed.

The couple didn't expect it because it was not a church program; the handbills didn't carry healing and deliverance sessions. Rather, what they wrote on it was emotional intelligence sessions with PJan and buffet, but that didn't stop them from keying into it to the glory of God.

My husband spoke with them and prayed. He told them God would visit them and, according to the time of life (which is within a year), they would have children. The couple looked at each other to ascertain the seriousness of those words. They were sceptical, but they believed even though that was the first time we were meeting. A year later, she gave birth to twins, two beautiful babies. Glory to God! After years of waiting; something that had not happened before happened by the power of God! God is awesome and He delights in blessing us.

Elizabeth, Mary's cousin, said, *"Blessed is she who believed, for there will be a fulfilment of those things which were told her from the Lord."*

Hallelujah! Will you be like Mary and say, *"Be it unto me, Lord, according to thy word."*

God has grand plans for your life *"For I know the thoughts that I think toward you, says the Lord, thoughts of peace, and not of evil, to give you an expected end."* Jer 29:11

Trust God with your life, have faith in Him. **"Without faith, it is impossible to please God"** *Heb11:6. Your* faith is important. Dare to believe in God and there shall be a performance of his plans and provisions for you. God is faithful, capable, and good. God is enough. Accept God's vision of a beautiful life for you and take steps fearlessly. Your faith is the victory that overcomes the world. Unbelieving takes as much work as believing, yet it produces no rewards; you do well to believe in God's goodness, power and faithfulness.

What women want

- Women want opportunities.
- Women want you to see their value.
- Women want to decide for themselves.
- Women want peace and justice.
- Women want to contribute.
- Women want appreciation.

Women respond to love and respect rather than coercion. The average woman is not as afraid as people like to think. Fear hardly stops women from doing anything they set their minds to do, even cheating on their spouses. A woman stays faithful more out of love and strong moral values than fear.

Women are very brave. That is why, despite little support, we rise every day and take what we want. Imagine all the good we would do if we had more support, understanding and opportunities.

Women are stronger than many people give them credit for. If men were the ones with menstrual cycles, they may not achieve half the things women achieve. I believe they may have passed a law that allows them to have 2weeks of paid holiday once every month, to allow them to recover from the hormonal changes.

Tips For Men

- One woman can give you all the love you need. Your wife is probably more interesting, multifaceted, attractive and intelligent than you give her credit for. Remember, you chose her. There must have been something amazing that made you settle with her. Your wife can be a worthy companion if you take a very good look at her. But if you ignore her, you may not know how soothing it is to enjoy a genuine friendship with someone so close. Your wife is the major stakeholder in your life; your every decision affects her more than everybody else. Someone may have indoctrinated you to look for love and friendship in the wrong places, but such a mindset can lead to errors. You may even think you do not need love. Some people thought so until they started having illicit affairs. Do not be proud; there is a craving in virtually everyone to be loved, needed and honoured. The Lord God said, "*It is not good for the man to be alone. I will make a helper suitable for him.*" Gen 2:18 NIV

This is a faithful saying: If a man desires the position of a bishop, he desires a good work. A bishop then must be blameless, the husband of one wife, temperate, sober-minded, of good behaviour, hospitable, able to teach; not given to wine, not violent, not greedy for money, but gentle, not quarrelsome, not covetous; one who rules his own house well, having his children in submission with all reverence (for if a man does not know how to rule his own house, how will he take care of the church of God?); not a novice, lest being puffed up with pride he fall into the same condemnation as the devil. Moreover he must have a good testimony among those who are outside, lest he fall into reproach and the snare of the devil. 1 Tim 3:1-7

- When a woman tells you another woman does not like her and disrespects her, do not be quick to say it is untrue. Women have ways to slight each other without the man knowing, even if they were standing right in front of him. They can assault each other by a gesture, a look or a sentence that appears harmless to a man. The Women's Code of Animosity is not readable by most men. So, don't get involved speedily else you may support the wrong party.

- There is such a thing as "a good woman" or a "bad woman". Sadly, though, when some men want to get married, they hardly consider the moral standards of the women. If you marry someone that does not care about honesty, loyalty and kindness, do not think your wedding ring on her finger is going to automatically input those virtues. (Some women also make this error). Pray for God's guidance before choosing a spouse. The bible says;

> *House and wealth are inherited from fathers,*
> *but a prudent wife is from the Lord.* Prov 19:14 ESV

- Protect the gift of trust, cherish it, because once broken, you may have to earn it; your partner may not give it freely like the first time. Sometimes this can be a problem because if you demand to be trusted, you are simply telling your partner to feign selective amnesia or play the fool. Every relationship is unique, so, while this may work for some, it may not work for others. The fool-proof strategy is - do not demand to be trusted without deciding to be trustworthy. Only an unwise person will submit to that.

- Respect women. Men who underestimate women do so at their own risk. You cannot intimidate a woman into submission. If you could, God would have asked you to. He didn't because, as the creator, He knows you can get a woman to submit by loving her.

Many people do not know what weaker vessels mean. Heads up please, not having equal muscle mass does not mean being undeserving of honour or being incapable of sound judgement.

Husbands, likewise, dwell with them with understanding, giving honor to the wife, as to the weaker vessel, and as being heirs together of the grace of life, that your prayers may not be hindered. Finally, all of you be of one mind, having compassion for one another; love as brothers, be tenderhearted, be courteous; not returning evil for evil or reviling for reviling, but on the contrary blessing, knowing that you were called to this, that you may inherit a blessing. 1 Peter 3:7-10

- The bible gave both the husband and wife roles. Sometimes either or both parties abdicate from their roles and still demand that their partner fulfill theirs. It is hypocritical to clamour for love and respect if you do not give it.

And further, submit to one another out of reverence for Christ. For wives, this means submit your husbands as to the Lord. For a husband is the head of his wife as Christ is the head of the church. He is the Saviour of his body, the church. As the church submits to Christ, so you wives should submit to your husbands in everything. For husbands, this means love your wives, just as Christ loved the church. He gave up his life for her to make her holy and clean, washed by the cleansing of God's word. He did this to present her to himself as a glorious church without a spot or wrinkle or any other blemish. Instead, she will be holy and without fault. In the same way, husbands ought to love their wives as they love their own bodies. For a man who loves his wife actually shows love for himself. No one hates his own body but feeds and cares for it, just as Christ cares for the church. And we are members of his body. As the Scriptures say, "A man leaves his father and mother and is joined to his wife, and the two are united into one." This is a great mystery, but it is an illustration of the way Christ and the church are one. So again I say, each man must love his wife as he loves himself, and the wife must respect her husband." Eph 5:21-33 TLB

- Talk about your expectations and find out if your definition of love aligns. A man said to his ex-girlfriend, "I love you, Agnes". Agnes said, "Your love is hurtful, if this is love I want none of it".

Every way of a man is right in his own eyes, but the Lord weighs the heart. To do righteousness and justice is more acceptable to the Lord than sacrifice. Prov 21:2-3

Dealing with marital problems?

- The first piece of advice you may get as an embattled husband is, "Show her who is boss, dominate her and withdraw support". Think very well before you follow that advice, because a neglected woman often turns into an uncontrollable woman. Your actions may break the bridge that holds you together. Remember, it is easier to destroy than to build.

- The second is, "Replace her or get her busy with a competitor; make her humble by giving her a rival. Whoever said polygamy was bad probably did not like men. Cheating is a matter of survival; get a side chick and get your peace". Okay, I believe you when you say your wife is quarrelsome. I understand your struggles because even the bible says, *"It is better to live in a corner of the housetop than in a house shared with a quarrelsome wife".* Prov 21:9 ESV. Yes, something has to be done, but not adultery, because it will not give you peace. Polygamy will not give you rest. Rather, communication may - ask yourself pertinent questions like - what are her grievances? And then tell her she needs to change her attitude. You can also consider taking couples' therapy.

Whoever commits adultery with a woman lacks understanding; He who does so destroys his own soul. Wounds and dishonour he will get, And his reproach will not be wiped away. Prov 6:32-33

And Pharisees came up to him and tested him by asking, "Is it lawful to divorce one's wife for any cause?" He answered, "Have you not read that he who created them from the beginning made them male and female, and said, 'Therefore a man shall leave his father and his mother and hold fast to his wife, and they shall become one flesh'? So they are no longer two but one flesh. What therefore God has joined together, let not man separate." They said to him, "Why then did Moses command one to give a certificate of divorce and to send her away?" He said to them, "Because of your hardness of heart Moses allowed you to divorce your wives, but from the beginning it was not so. And I say to you: whoever divorces his wife, except for sexual immorality, and marries another, commits adultery." Matt 19:3-9 ESV

- The third is, "Love your wife". This may seem like the hardest, especially if there has been a lot of rancour. But it is the most likely solution to your problem because women love to be loved and most will reciprocate your love until you are dizzy from love. Most, not all, because few people have a mental limitation or character flaw; they do not know how to respond to love.

Be mindful of third parties, but never be ashamed to seek the right counsel. Prov 11:14, *For lack of guidance, a nation falls, but many advisers make victory sure.* NIV

Be encouraged: 1 Cor 13:8 says love never fails.

- Kindness is a quick fix for most relationship challenges. But to their detriment, some men have turned their angels into demons, and some women have turned their gentlemen into beasts. You, be wise; be a good person. It is the best gift you can give yourself. Let no one make a monster out of you.

   A man who is kind benefits himself,
   but a cruel man hurts himself. ESV Prov 11:17

Virtuous woman

A virtuous woman is a woman who lives her life displaying virtues. Virtues refer to moral excellence, chastity and commendable attributes that promote goodness and glorify God. A virtuous woman is a woman of noble character, full of abilities and capabilities.

"Who can find a virtuous woman? For her price is far above rubies. The heart of her husband doth safely trust in her, so that he shall have no need of spoil. She will do him good and not evil all the days of her life . She seeks wool, and flax, and works willingly with her hands. She is like the merchants' ships; she brings her food from afar. She rises also while it is yet night, and gives meat to her household, and a portion to her maidens. She considers a field, and buys it: with the fruit of her hands, she plants a vineyard. She girds her loins with strength, and strengthens her arms.

She perceives that her merchandise is good: her candle goes not out by night. She lays her hands to the spindle, and her hands hold the distaff. She stretches out her hand to the poor; yea, she reaches forth her hands to the needy. She is not afraid of the snow for her household: for all her household are clothed with scarlet. She makes herself coverings of tapestry; her clothing is silk and purple. Her husband is known in the gates, when he sits among the elders of the land. She makes fine linen, and sells it; and delivers girdles unto the merchant. Strength and honour are her clothing; and she shall rejoice in time to come. She opens her mouth with wisdom; and in her tongue is the law of kindness.

*   She looks well to the ways of her household, and eat not the bread of idleness. Her children arise up, and call her blessed; her husband also, and he praises her. Many daughters have done virtuously, but thou excel them all. Favour is deceitful, and beauty is vain: but a woman that fears the Lord, she shall be praised. Give her of the fruit of her hands and let her own works praise her in the gates. "* Prov 31:10-31 KJV

In today's world, who is a virtuous woman?

A virtuous woman is a jewel of inestimable value.
A virtuous woman is a confident woman;
She knows her worth.
A virtuous is a woman you can trust.
She is full of good works; she is industrious.
She is responsible.
She is self-motivated, she is a goal-getter.
She is enterprising.
She plans ahead.
She is caring.
She is strong.
She dresses elegantly.
She is wise and discerning.
Her husband is honourable.
She is honourable.
She is a good home manager.

She is that woman who fears the Lord.
She is the woman that likes to contribute.
A virtuous woman is a value-adding woman.

Like a gold ring in a pig's snout is a beautiful woman without discretion. Prov 11:22 ESV

A virtuous woman is you, me and every woman who meets these criteria. She is not a legend; she is not a myth that needs busting; she is not just a character in some fables. Virtuous women are real and they abound.

It is easy to be virtuous because no matter where you are, all it takes is a simple decision to work in the grace, love and power of God.

Some were born virtuous - I know a lot of women with no stain on their lives, no mean streak or sordid past, pure as a babe even after many years. They didn't fall to rise. They never hurt anyone or soiled their hands. Do not be ashamed if you fall into this category. You are as valid as the one who learnt obedience after being disobedient; you don't need to have lived sinfully to teach others God's Word.

Some became virtuous - I have met women who rose above their sordid past to become paragons of virtue. I applaud the faith of women who rose from the ashes and are inspiring others to come up hither, "there's room at the top". Their testimony of coming into Christ after having experienced sin and darkness is a great evangelical tool, though not a standard criterion for every witness.

Many more are becoming virtuous - I see many willing to rise and be counted as virtuous women. To these women, I say don't dwell on your mistakes. You can become a better version of yourself. That you are on this path of self-discovery and development means your victory is certain.

A gracious woman retains honour, But ruthless men retain riches. Prov 11:16

All the women who had ability and were wise-hearted spun with their hands and brought what they had spun of blue and purple and scarlet [stuff] and fine linen; And all the women who had ability and whose hearts stirred them up in wisdom spun the goats' hair. Ex 35:25-26 AMP

Elizabeth

Elizabeth is the wife of Zacharias, the cousin of virgin Mary and the mother of John the Baptist.

*"Now indeed, Elizabeth your relative has also conceived a son in her old age; and this is now the sixth month for her who was called barren. For with God nothing will be impossible."*Luke 1:36-37

She conceived a son in her old age. Verse 36, makes me shout for joy. The bible said this is the sixth month with her, who was called "barren," notice it didn't say with *her "who was barren."* There is a big difference between being "**called**" something and being something.

What men call you is irrelevant; the important thing is what God calls you. It's all about God's plan because, with God, nothing is impossible. Studying scriptures shows us that nothing is new. Men have been branding people and trying to call each other names that God did not call them.

Oh, how much I love it when God shows up. I love the way He turns the wisdom of men into foolishness. I love the way He changes the story and turns the one who was called barren into a mother. I love the way he takes away the shame and renames us for beauty and glory.

Elizabeth is a kind, discerning woman who is yielded to the spirit of God. See what happens when Mary visited her...

> *"When Elizabeth heard Mary's greeting, the baby in her womb leaped. She was filled with the Holy Spirit, and sang out exuberantly, you're so blessed among women and the babe in your womb, also blessed! And why am I so blessed that the mother of my Lord visits me?*
>
> *The moment the sound of your greeting entered my ears, The babe in my womb skipped like a lamb for sheer joy. Blessed woman, who believed what God said, believed every word would come true!* Luke 1:41-45

<u>Elizabeth was a good and godly woman</u>. Only a good person would be humble enough to accept that her contemporary had something she didn't and then announce it to her. It takes a different level of faith to prophesy the way Elizabeth did – she called Mary the mother of her Lord. Some people have refused to prophesy to friends just because the glory of their testimony is grander than theirs. Elizabeth wasn't instructed to act honourably towards Mary. Her behaviour expressed her selfless, beautiful heart. The Bible didn't record that an angel visited Elizabeth, yet she responded like she was there when Angel Gabriel spoke to Mary. The Holy Spirit has free expression where there is no strife. Truth is, only a spirit-filled woman can prophesy the Word of God to another woman like that. Elizabeth is a supporter, a true sister and friend; with people like that, your life is sweeter.

Look at Mary's response after listening to Elizabeth;

And Mary said: "My soul magnifies the Lord, And my spirit has rejoiced in God my Saviour. For He has regarded the lowly state of His maidservant; For behold, henceforth all generations will call me blessed. For He who is mighty has done great things for me, And holy is His name. And His mercy is on those who fear Him from generation to generation. Luke 1:46-50

See, Mary was further strengthened after hearing from Elizabeth. Mary had to be around Elizabeth. She needed to hear her! No wonder Angel Gabriel told Mary about her; it was so Mary would go visiting. Praise God!

I cannot emphasise this enough; it is a blessing to have good friends and be around women who are not afraid to speak God's words of blessing over you. Such beautiful and empowering words like the ones Elizabeth uttered can only come from a heart free of rivalry, pretence and competition; they could only be inspired by love.

Some women have miscarried and aborted their blessings because of the wrong people; people who don't realise there is no need for comparisons. After all, we all work in preordained paths. Life is about predestination - nothing could turn Elizabeth into Mary. We all have our roles laid out for us. As we work with love, the blessings and beauty of God unfold before us, so celebrate with others, thank God for their success and thank Him for yours.

"And Mary remained with her about three months and returned to her house. Now Elizabeth's full time came for her to be delivered, and she brought forth a son. When her neighbours and relatives heard

how the Lord had shown great mercy to her, they rejoiced with her,"
Luke 1:56-58.

In accomplishing our destinies, we all need discerning, spirit-filled and supportive friends/cousins/sisters like Elizabeth. And the easiest way to get such friends is to become such a friend; be to others what you want them to be to you.

Every woman deserves to have a good friend.

Mary (The Sister Of Lazarus And Martha)

His Mary was the Sister of Lazarus and Martha. This Mary was the woman who broke an alabaster box of ointment to honour the Lord.

Now one of the Pharisees invited Jesus to have dinner with him, so he went to the Pharisee's house and reclined at the table. When a woman who had lived a sinful life in that town learned that Jesus was eating at the Pharisee's house, she brought an alabaster jar of perfume, and as she stood behind him at his feet weeping, she began to wet his feet with her tears. Then she wiped them with her hair, kissed them and poured perfume on them. When the Pharisee who had invited him saw this, he said to himself, "If this man were a prophet, he would know who is touching him and what kind of woman she is — that she is a sinner." Luke 7:36-39NIV.

One of the first lessons I gleaned from the life of Mary is the power of worship. Worship is love and deep honour intertwined; you cannot worship what you don't love. Just the way you have a craving for love, God wants your worship. He doesn't tire of or reject heartfelt worship. Genuine worship can put you in the right standing with God.

From reading the above scripture, I saw Mary as a repentant woman, but the people referred to her as a sinner. I like to call such people the sinner detectors; they seem to have a record of others' sins and they never forget even after God has forgiven. The Pharisee who invited Jesus Christ home dared question the divinity of Jesus because Jesus allowed Mary to touch Him. You can just imagine the scorn, disgust and anger her presence must have caused. Yet she shunned it all. Only one thing was on her mind, the worship of the Master. Despite the people's attitude, she went ahead to offer her sacrifice.

Look sister, there will always be people who will feel that you don't qualify to worship God or be used by Him. They think they know you; they love to emphasize your mistakes and they never want to let go of your past. Ignore them; don't wait for people to validate you before you serve God and fulfill your destiny in Christ. They may never accredit you, especially if they are narrow-minded or have a superiority complex.

There will always be people who will think you give too much, or you go to church too often. When you decide to serve the Lord, you may meet people like Judas who think we should not give the Lord all the praise we know we should give to Him. Never listen to them!

So, did you date the wrong man? Or are you divorced? Or did you have a child out of wedlock? Or did you have an abortion? Or did you lie? Or did you steal? The answers to these questions don't matter. What matters is the answer to these: have you repented? Have you received the salvation Jesus brought? Have you given your life to Christ? Are you born again? Have you received the Holy Spirit?

If you want to give your life to Jesus Christ, read these Bible passages, say the prayer and mean it.

Jesus answered and said to him, "Most assuredly, I say to you, unless one is born again, he cannot see the kingdom of God. Do not marvel that I said to you, 'You must be born again.' John 3:3,7

For God so loved the world that He gave His only begotten Son, that whoever believes in Him should not perish but have everlasting life. For God did not send His Son into the world to condemn the world, but that the world through Him might be saved. "He who believes in Him is not condemned; but he who does not believe is condemned already because he has not believed in the name of the only begotten Son of God. And this is the condemnation, that the light has come into the world, and men loved darkness rather than light, because their deeds were evil. For everyone practicing evil hates the light and does not come to the light, lest his deeds should be exposed.   But he who does the truth comes to the light, that his deeds may be clearly seen, that they have been done in God. "John 3:16-21

" that if you confess with your mouth the Lord Jesus and believe in your heart that God has raised Him from the dead, you will be saved. For with the heart one believes unto righteousness, and with the mouth, confession is made unto salvation. For the Scripture says, "Whoever believes on Him will not be put to shame Rom 10:9-11 .

"Nor is there salvation in any other, for there is no other name under heaven given among men by which we must be saved." Acts 4:12

"He who believes in the Son of God has the witness in himself; he who does not believe God has made Him a liar, because he has not believed the testimony that God has given of His Son. And this is the testimony: that God has given us eternal life, and this life is in His Son. He who has the Son has life; he who does not have the

Son of God does not have life. 1 John 5:10-12

Prayer of salvation

Dear Lord Jesus, I come to you just as I am. I believe with all my heart that you are the Son of the living God. I believe you died for my sins and God raised you from the dead. I repent of my sins today and I confess your lordship over my life. I receive eternal life and I declare you are my Lord and Saviour. I'm born-again. Thank you, dear Lord Jesus, for saving my soul. I am a child of God. Amen!

...Listen once you repent and accept the Lordship of Jesus Christ. It is a new you. This new you are free to live, love and serve God.

The Samaritan woman moved from being the woman that had five husbands and a live-in relationship to an Evangelist; when you meet Jesus, that's what happens. The shame, pain and reproach are gone. Your broken heart gets mended, your past is gone and in its wake is a vibrant zeal to serve God. It invigorates you to embark on a mission to tell others about the goodness of the Lord. Once saved, you can't keep this joy and peace to yourself or hide the fact that you are enjoying new freedom from the dead weight of guilt and condemnation... Yes, once you are liberated, you want to see others liberated too.

And she had a sister called <u>Mary</u>, who also sat at Jesus' feet and heard His word. Luke 10:39-40 She here refers to Martha. While Martha was encumbered by many things, Mary sat at the master's feet. Another thing to note about Mary is her love for fellowship; she would rather sit and hear the Word of God than do anything else.

> *"Now a certain man was sick, named Lazarus, of Bethany, the town of Mary and her sister Martha. (It was that Mary which anointed the Lord with ointment, and wiped his feet with her hair, whose brother Lazarus was sick.)"* John 11:1-2 (KJV)

> *<u>Then, when Mary came where Jesus was, and saw Him, she fell down at His feet,</u> saying to Him, "Lord, if You had been here, my brother would not have died."* John 11:32 NKJV

Notice the underlined sentence, Mary was a worshipper, worshippers stir God and have supernatural results. When Martha saw Jesus, she didn't worship, she went straight to the point and somewhat accusingly said, "Lord if you had been here my brother would not have died". Little wonder she had a conversation with the Lord without a change. Mary said the same words Martha did, but with a different attitude. Mary could fall at Jesus' feet; be vulnerable and share her grief because she was humble. Humility precedes worship and surrender.

> *When Jesus saw her weeping, and the Jews who had come with her also weeping, he was deeply moved in his spirit and greatly troubled. And he said, "Where have you laid him?"* John 11:33-34 ESV.

We all know how the story ended - Lazarus was resurrected. The right attitude makes so much difference. Tender your request with understanding. Approach the Lord with Worship. Fall on your knees, lay at His feet.

The Woman of Samaria

There came a woman of Samaria to draw water. Jesus said to her, "Give Me a drink." For His disciples had gone away into the city to buy food. Therefore the Samaritan woman said to Him, "How is it that You, being a Jew, ask me for a drink since I am a Samaritan woman?" (For Jews have no dealings with Samaritans.)

The first lesson here is about how segregation, racism, ethnicism and denominationalism can stop us from getting the best of God and enjoying genuine relationships. Did you notice how she responded when the Lord asked her to give him water? She probably wondered about where he had been or what kind of person He was. And when she couldn't hide her perplexity or ignore her curiosity, she blatantly asked Him why He was asking for water from her. How many times have we missed our blessings because it came in a different package from what we classify as familiar or who we term worthy? Our Lord Jesus is so gracious and kind. He explained to her. . . .

Jesus answered and said to her, "If you knew the gift of God, and who it is who says to you, 'Give Me a drink,' you would have asked Him, and He would have given you living water." She said to Him, " Sir, You have nothing to draw with and the well is deep; where then do You get that living water? "You are not greater than our father Jacob, are You, who gave us the well, and drank of it himself and his sons and his cattle?" Jesus answered and said to her, "Everyone who drinks of this water will thirst again; but whoever drinks of the water that I will give him shall never thirst; but the water that I will give him will become in him a well of water springing up to eternal life." The woman said to Him, " Sir, give me this water, so I will not be thirsty nor come all the way here to draw."

The compassion of Christ makes me awestruck. He was not interested in condemning her. Read on. . . .

He said to her, "Go, call your husband and come here." The woman answered and said, "I have no husband." Jesus said to her, "You have correctly said, 'I have no husband'; for you have had five husbands, and the one whom you now have is not your husband; this you have said truly."

There's a difference between a husband and a lover. What do you think is the difference between the five that were called husbands and the one who was not?

The woman said to Him, "Sir, I perceive that You are a prophet." Our fathers worshiped in this mountain, and you people say that in Jerusalem is the place where men ought to worship." Jesus said to her, "Woman, believe Me, an hour is coming when neither in this mountain nor in Jerusalem will you worship the Father. You worship what you do not know; we worship what we know, for salvation is from the Jews. But an hour is coming, and now is, when the true worshipers will worship the Father in spirit and truth; for such people the Father seeks to be His worshipers. God is spirit, and those who worship Him must worship in spirit and truth." The woman said to Him,

"I know that Messiah is coming (He who is called Christ); when that One comes, He will declare all things to us." Jesus said to her, " I who speak to you am He."

Our Lord Jesus told her about what true worship was. He also told her that He was the Christ.

> *At this point His disciples came, and they were amazed that He had been speaking with a woman, yet no one said, "What do You seek?" or, "Why do You speak with her?" So the woman left her waterpot, and went into the city and said to the men, "Come, see a man who told me all the things that I have done; this is not the Christ, is it?" They went out of the city, and were coming to Him.* John 4:7-30 NASU

God cares about everyone, Jews, Samaritans, Gentiles, male or female. Jesus had a riveting conversation with the Samaritan woman. He talked to her with dignity. He opened her eyes to see what was really important – the living water only Him could give, which is symbolic of eternal life, peace, joy and fulfilment– that does not provide only momentary satisfaction. No wonder she went to preach to others the moment she left the well.

For those who think women should not preach, evangelize or be actively involved in gathering people to God's kingdom, this should make you change your mind. The disciples were probably shocked when they saw the Lord talking to her, not just because He was talking to a woman, but because it was similar to the way He talked with them. He revealed the truth to her. He answered her questions and dissolved her doubts. He was grooming her to be sent. They could tell it was strategic, it was the making of a female evangelist; they were surprised she was being discipled to be sent! The Lord's response in the preceding verses shows that this was a pivotal moment that had a lot to do with the harvest. It was all about the work.

Meanwhile the disciples were urging him, "Rabbi, eat something." But he said to them, "I have food to eat that you know nothing about." So the disciples began to say to one another, "No one brought him anything to eat, did they?" Jesus said to them, <u>"My food is to do the will of the one who sent me and to complete his work</u>. Don't you say, 'There are four more months and then comes the harvest?' I tell you, look up and see that the fields are already white for harvest! The one who reaps receives pay and gathers fruit for eternal life, so that the one who sows and the one who reaps can rejoice together. For in this instance the saying is true, 'One sows and another reaps.' I sent you to reap what you did not work for; others have labored and you have entered into their labor." John 4:31-38

He refused to eat because He was waiting for her. And true to His plans, she went out and publicised the gospel. The bible says many believed because of her words. She – a woman, was the person whom Jesus Christ used to announce His Presence and send His message across Samaria.

From that city many of the Samaritans believed in Him because of the word of the woman who testified, "He told me all the things that I have done." So when the Samaritans came to Jesus, they were asking Him to stay with them; and He stayed there two days. Many more believed because of His word; and they were saying to the woman, "It is no longer because of what you said that we believe, for we have heard for ourselves and know that this One is indeed the Savior of the world." John 4:39-42 NASU

The Samaritan woman's encounter with the Lord and her subsequent work proves that arguments about whether a woman ought to preach is needless. First off, what is preaching? Preaching is simply sharing your knowledge of God's Word; telling others about the impact of God's Word on your life and revealing the promises of God for their life. When talking about preaching, from this passage, we can know that gender and past experiences should disqualify no one. Everyone can and should preach about the grace, mercy, power and love of God.

Michal

M ichal was a princess. She was the daughter of Saul and the first wife of David.

Though Michal was in love with David, that was not Saul's primary reason for giving her to him. Saul wanted to use his daughter to destroy David.

> Then Saul said to David, "Here is my elder daughter Merab. I will give her to you for a wife. Only be valiant for me and fight the Lord's battles." For Saul thought, "Let not my hand be against him, but let the hand of the Philistines be against him." And David said to Saul, "Who am I, and who are my relatives, my father's clan in Israel, that I should be son-in-law to the king?" But at the time when Merab, Saul's daughter, should have been given to David, she was given to Adriel the Meholathite for a wife.

> Now Saul's daughter Michal loved David. And they told Saul, and the thing pleased him. Saul thought, "Let me give her to him, that she may be a snare for him and that the hand of the Philistines may be against him." Therefore Saul said to David a second time, "You shall now be my son-in-law." And Saul commanded his servants, "Speak to David in private and say, 'Behold, the king has delight in you, and all his servants love

you. Now then become the king's son-in-law." And Saul's servants spoke those words in the ears of David. And David said, "Does it seem to you a little thing to become the king's son-in-law, since I am a poor man and have no reputation?"

And the servants of Saul told him, "So did David speak." Then Saul said, "Thus shall you say to David, 'The king desires no bride-price except a hundred foreskins of the Philistines, that he may be avenged of the king's enemies." Now Saul thought to make David fall by the hand of the Philistines. And when his servants told David these words, it pleased David well to be the king's son-in-law. Before the time had expired, David arose and went, along with his men, and killed two hundred of the Philistines. And David brought their foreskins, which were given in full number to the king, that he might become the king's son-in-law. And Saul gave him his daughter Michal for a wife. But when Saul saw and knew that the Lord was with David, and that Michal, Saul's daughter, loved him, Saul was even more afraid of David. So Saul was David's enemy continually. 1 Sam 18:17-29 ESV

David did nothing to deserve Saul's enmity. Saul just hated him for being fabulous. The thought that there was a man who could be greater than him seemed to unleash demons in Saul. When caught in a web of envy between people you love, and you have to take a side, what do you do? Michal didn't act ignorant or lie that her father's animosity was all a figment of David's imagination.

Saul also sent messengers to David's house to watch him and to kill him in the morning. And Michal, David's wife, told him, saying, "If you do not save your life tonight, tomorrow you will be killed." So Michal let David down through a window. And he went and fled and escaped. And Michal took an image and laid it in the bed, put a cover of goats' hair for his head, and covered it with clothes. So when Saul sent messengers to take David, she said, "He is sick."

Then Saul sent the messengers back to see David, saying, "Bring him up to me in the bed, that I may kill him." And when the messengers had come in, there was the image in the bed, with a cover of goats' hair for his head. Then Saul said to Michal, "Why have you deceived me like this, and sent my enemy away, so that he has escaped?" And Michal answered Saul, "He said to me, 'Let me go! Why should I kill you?" 1 Sam 19:11-17

Michal saved David, her husband's life. She was not in denial about her father's bad intentions for David. I do not know if Saul believed her feigned helplessness or recognised her loyalty to David, but at some point, he got her married to someone else.

Saul had given Michal his daughter, David's wife, to Palti the son of Laish, who was of Gallim. 1 Sam 25:44. ESV

After Saul died in battle, David requested to have his wife back as a condition of his negotiation with Abner.

Then Abner sent messengers to David, saying, "Doesn't the entire land belong to you? Make a solemn pact with me, and I will help turn over all of Israel to you."

"All right," David replied, "but I will not negotiate with you unless you bring back my wife Michal, Saul's daughter, when you come." David then sent this message to Ishbosheth, Saul's son: "Give me back my wife Michal, for I bought her with the lives of 100 Philistines." So Ishbosheth took Michal away from her husband, Palti

son of Laish. Palti followed along behind her as far as Bahurim, weeping as he went. Then Abner told him, "Go back home!" So Palti returned. 2 Sam 3:12-16 NLT

What a dramatic marriage, but that was not the end. The next series of events changed what may have been a joyous reunion. We are likely to make the mistake Michal made if we forget the position of God.

"Now as the ark of the Lord came into the City of David, Michal, Saul's daughter, looked through a window and saw King David leaping and whirling before the Lord; and she despised him in her heart. So they brought the ark of the Lord, and set it in its place in the midst of the tabernacle that David had erected for it. Then David offered burnt offerings and peace offerings before the Lord. And when David had finished offering burnt offerings and peace offerings, he blessed the people in the name of the Lord of hosts. Then he distributed among all the people, among the whole multitude of Israel, both the women and the men, to everyone a loaf of bread, a piece of meat, and a cake of raisins. So, all the people departed, everyone to his house. Then David returned to bless his household.

And Michal the daughter of Saul came out to meet David, and said, "How glorious was the king of Israel today, uncovering himself today in the eyes of the maids of his servants, as one of the base fellows shamelessly uncovers himself!" So David said to Michal, "It was before the Lord, who chose me instead of your father and all his house, to appoint me ruler over the people of the Lord, over Israel. Therefore I will play music before the Lord. And I will be even more undignified than this, and will be humble in my own sight. But as for the maidservants of whom you have *spoken, by them I will be held in honour." Therefore Michal the daughter of Saul had no children to the day of her death".*2 Sam 6:16-23

Michal came across as a proud woman who was ignorant of spiritual things. Ignorance, though, has never been a good defence, so she paid dearly for her arrogance.

When Michal saw her husband dancing unto the Lord; she misunderstood and misinterpreted it for debauchery. As a woman, you will do yourself a great favour when you know you cannot compete with God. Everything is not about you.

God is in control of everything, even your husband. You are not in the same class as Him and so can never be rivals. Thus, it is foolhardy to act as if you are in a contest over your husband's love, attention, affection and finances with God.

Michal felt humiliated by her husband's humble display of honour and gratitude towards God in front of everyone. Some women feel irritated when they see their husbands bow before God. Some women hate to see their husbands give for church projects, honour their pastors, serve in church or help people. It is not right to act like such a woman. The biblical account of God's response towards Michal shows us how God feels about it.

God is our strength, joy, restorer and beautifier - if a wife plays down on God's word and authority in her home, who will she turn to the day she needs a supernatural intervention? If her husband ever does something wrong, in her pride she won't be able to talk to God because she has always disregarded His authority and she probably cannot tell her pastor to pray or counsel with them; since she has always told her husband to ignore him.

Years back, a young couple was having intense marital issues because the husband somehow got addicted to pornography. Also, he was having a strange relationship with his female colleagues.

One day, he asked his wife to move out and stay out. She tried talking to him, to no avail. Many family meetings had no positive effect. Then she remembered, "Ah-ha, the pastor is a good man. My husband respects our pastor. He is like a son to the pastor. He will listen to pastor". So, she spoke to her pastor about it. The pastor then asked her husband to see him. They had a meeting, and he spoke to him about the dangers of pornography and boundary-less relationship with the opposite sex; it always leads to emotional cheating and subsequently adultery. It was a long meeting but praise be to God! That was the end of marital struggles for that young couple.

When you submit your family to the grace of God, honouring Him comes naturally, and God will reward your honour.

Live for God and serve Him, even if others like Michal think it is undignified. Truth is, everyone serves something, and everyone bows to something. Some people worship themselves and will go to strange lengths to satisfy themselves... you do well to choose to serve God, continue happily and unashamedly because no one knows like you do what He has done for you.

The bible says Palti cried and followed Michal as she was being taken to David. We do not know how Michal's relationship with

Palti was before David commanded to have her brought to him. Could it be that she was sarcastic and resentful of David because she had grown attached to Palti? I felt touched by Michal's error because she was a good wife to David. It could have been a happy ending and her son might have been a king. She started well, but her dad tried to break her loyalty to David and thus probably complicated her life. May nothing corrupt our rewards and harvest of blessings.

Are you so foolish? Having begun by the Spirit, are you now being perfected by the flesh? Gal 3:3 ESV

Primary guide on women's roles

Daughter	What does it mean to be a daughter in the 21st century? What does it mean to be a Christian unmarried lady? What is expected of you? *"That our daughters may be as pillars, Sculptured in palace style;"* Ps 144:12 A daughter is a source of joy to her family, an object of love and praise with the responsibility to be herself; help around the house and provide whatever support she can give. A daughter's greatest responsibility is to learn the right things, be happy and grow to be a blessing to her family.
Wife	*"In the same way, you wives must accept the authority of your husbands. Then, even if some refuse to obey the Good News, your godly lives*

	will speak to them without any words. They will be won over by observing your pure and reverent lives. Don't be concerned about the outward beauty of fancy hairstyles, expensive jewellery, or beautiful clothes. *You should clothe yourselves instead with the beauty that comes from within, the unfading beauty of a gentle and quiet spirit, which is so precious to God. This is how the holy women of old made themselves beautiful. They trusted God and accepted the authority of their husbands. For instance, Sarah obeyed her husband, Abraham, and called him her master. You are her daughters when you do what is right without fear of what your husbands might do.* 1 Peter 3:1-6 A wife's responsibility is to love her husband and children and do what's best for them. A wife is to respect her husband and yet relate without fear towards him.
Mother	The mother is the first role model, the nurturer, the caregiver and supporter. The scriptures highlight the duties and responsibilities of a mother. *"Older women likewise are to exhibit behaviour fitting for those who are holy, not slandering, not slaves to excessive drinking, but teaching what is good. In this way they will*

	train the younger women to love their husbands, to love their children, to be self-controlled, pure, fulfilling their duties at home, kind, being subject to their own husbands, so that the message of God may not be discredited. Titus 2:3-5 NET Mothers should be honoured and loved; *"Honour your father and your mother, that your days may be long upon the land which the Lord your God is giving you.* Ex 20:12 *Listen with respect to the father who raised you, <u>and when your mother grows old, don't neglect her.</u>* Prov 23:22MSB. *Let your father and your mother be glad, And let her who bore you rejoice.* Prov 23:25.
Sister	*"Love wisdom like a sister; make insight a beloved member of your family. Let them protect you from an affair with an immoral woman, from listening to the flattery of a promiscuous woman.* Prov 7:4-5NLT *"* This scripture gives us an insight into the role of a sister. A sister is to be loved; because a sister is there to protect. In this part of the world, we find that a lot of sisters love to play the role of protectors albeit

without knowledge. Stories of controlling sisters turning sisters-in-law who have destroyed families in their bid to protect them are too many to be ignored. The role of a sister is sensitive, hence, the need for selflessness, truth and understanding cannot be over-emphasised. Zeal without knowledge leads to destruction.

Look at how a proactive sister, saved her brothers generation and the people of Israel: *"But Jehosheba, the daughter of King Jehoram and sister of Ahaziah, took Joash son of Ahaziah and stole him away from among the royal princes, who were about to be murdered. She put him and his nurse in a bedroom to hide him from Athaliah; so he was not killed."*2 Kings 11:2NIV

Whenever I study about Jesus' visit to Martha's house, I replay the dynamics between the sisters in my imagination. Funnily enough, siblings reporting each other to a higher authority didn't start in your family. Also, feeling like a sibling is taking advantage of you, using you or disregarding you is not a new thing, as we saw the same thing play out in scripture: *"As Jesus and his disciples were on their way, he came to a village where a woman named Martha opened her home to him. She had a sister called Mary, who sat at the Lord's feet listening to what he said. But Martha was distracted by all the preparations that had to be made. She came to him and asked, "Lord, don't you care that my sister has left me to do the work by myself? Tell her to help me!"*

"Martha, Martha," the Lord answered, *"you are worried and upset about many things, but only one thing is needed. Mary has chosen what is better, and it will not be taken away from her."* Luke 10:38-42 NIV

A sister is someone you share a strong and yet pure bond with, *"...and treat younger women with all purity as you would your own sisters."* 1 Tim 5:2 NLT

I grew up noticing that most brothers always look out for their sisters, but I didn't know it was biblical till I read this: *"we have a little sister too young to have breasts. What will we do for our sister if someone asks to marry her? If she is a virgin, like a wall, we will protect her with a silver tower. But if she is promiscuous, like a swinging door, we will block her door with a cedar bar."* Song 8:8-9

Hannah

"There was a certain man from Ramathaim, a Zuphite from the hill country of Ephraim, whose name was Elkanah son of Jeroham, the son of Elihu, the son of Tohu, the son of Zuph, an Ephraimite. He had two wives; one was called Hannah and the other Peninnah. Peninnah had children, but Hannah had none." [1]
Sam 1:1-2 NIV

"Elkanah her husband would say to her, "Hannah, why are you weeping? Why don't you eat? Why are you downhearted? Don't I mean more to you than ten sons?"

LESSONS FROM HANNAH

Waiting to conceive is a very trying time for anyone. Elkanah, Hannah's husband, supported her during this season by treating her lovingly. He was generous to her and encouraged her. Whereas some men terrorize, blame and tell their wives they are worthless because they are yet to have children, Elkanah asked her, "Don't I mean more to you than many sons?"

Another thing worthy of note about Hannah was her not fighting Peninnah. When Hannah was mocked, she didn't respond with a quarrel... she didn't get aggressive or allow herself to be dragged into a hopeless exchange of toxic words. Rather, she did the best thing anyone in her situation could do - she turned to the Lord in prayer. She poured her heart out to God! She was so lost in tendering her petition that the priest observing her thought she was drunk. She made a vow to the Lord.

> *Once when they had finished eating and drinking in Shiloh, Hannah stood up. Now Eli the priest was sitting on a chair by the doorpost of the Lord's temple. In bitterness of soul Hannah wept much and prayed to the Lord.* <u>*And she made a vow, saying, "O Lord Almighty, if you will only look upon your servant's misery and remember me, and not forget your servant but give her a son, then I will give him to the Lord for all the days of his life, and no razor will ever be used on his head."*</u>*As she kept on praying to the Lord, Eli observed her mouth. Hannah was praying in her heart, and her lips were moving but her voice was not heard. Eli thought she was drunk and said to her, "How long will you keep on getting drunk? Get rid of your wine.""Not so, my lord," Hannah replied, "I am a woman who is deeply troubled. I have not been drinking wine or beer; I was pouring out my soul to the Lord. Do not take your servant for a wicked woman; I have been praying here out of my great anguish and grief."*<u>*Eli answered, "Go in peace, and may the God of Israel grant you what you have asked of him."*</u>

Hannah believed in GOD. After praying and getting a word of confirmation from Eli the prophet, the bible says Hannah said, *"May your servant find favour in your eyes."* <u>*Then she went her way and ate something, and her face was no longer downcast.*</u> *Early the next morning, they arose and worshipped before the Lord and then went back to their home at Ramah.*

71

Note the underlined sentence; her face was no longer downcast. Now, that is faith! She believed there was no longer cause for sadness. Are you one of the few people who prayed and got a response from God yet carried on as if they never prayed and He never answered? Please take a cue from Hannah.

Read and see how Hannah got her miracle and kept her word. She redeemed her vow; she took her son Samuel and gave him to the Lord as she had said. And the Lord blessed her with more children. Honouring our vow is so beautiful because God always out gives us.

Elkanah lay with Hannah his wife, and the Lord remembered her. So in the course of time Hannah conceived and gave birth to a son. She named him Samuel, saying, "Because I asked the Lord for him."

When the man Elkanah went up with all his family to offer the annual sacrifice to the Lord and to fulfill his vow, Hannah did not go. She said to her husband, "After the boy is weaned, I will take him and present him before the Lord, and he will live there always."

"Do what seems best to you," Elkanah her husband told her. "Stay here until you have weaned him; only may the Lord make good his word." So the woman stayed at home and nursed her son until she had weaned him.

After he was weaned, she took the boy with her, young as he was, along with a three-year-old bull, an ephah of flour and a skin of wine, and brought him to the house of the Lord at Shiloh. When they had slaughtered the bull, they brought the boy to Eli, and she said to him, "As surely as you live, my lord, I am the woman who stood here beside you praying to the Lord. I prayed for this child, and the Lord has granted me what I asked of him. So now I give him to the Lord. For his whole life he will be given over to the Lord." And he worshiped the Lord there." 1 Sam 1:8-28 NIV

"But Samuel was ministering before the Lord-a boy wearing a linen ephod. Each year his mother made him a little robe and took it to him when she went up with her husband to offer the annual sacrifice. Eli would bless Elkanah and his wife, saying, "May the Lord give you children by this woman to take the place of the one she prayed for and gave to the Lord." Then they would go home. <u>*And the Lord was gracious to Hannah; she conceived and gave birth to three sons and two daughters. Meanwhile, the boy Samuel grew up in the presence of the Lord."*</u> 1 Sam 2:18-21 NIV

Women Who Fight

Defining moments are hardly complete without the input of brave women. History is replete with tales of women who fought against injustice; women who fought for a new and better life.

I particularly love women who achieve great things without losing their feminine touch. I celebrate women who see their feminity as a strength and use it as a weapon, women who are never afraid because of their gender, women who don't just seek gender equality but harness the power in gender difference.

Understanding gender differences is a way to deal with gender inequality without making more women stifled and burdened.

A conversation with an uninformed feminist (u.f)

U.f: "She should be ashamed of herself. She is so stupid. Is her husband the only husband that has money, no matter what he has, who stays at home just to take care of their children? abi iru oshi wo lele yi (translation: what type of nonsense is that)... I am up by 4:00am to hustle, I don't ask my husband for anything...what a man can do a woman can do better," she bragged.

I smiled and wondered why we are holding women to the same mean and stereotypical standards men did.

To me, gender equality is the freedom of a woman to exercise the right to be in charge of her own life, to choose what she wants and how she wants to live with no one- whether male or female butting in and acting like they know what is best for her. Feminism is the right of a woman to be herself without abnormal demands and expectations. The right to live an honourable life as ordained by God, with God's Word as the standard. Because God cares about women, he created laws that protect women but wicked, cunning, insecure men have severally tried to misunderstand those laws and teach others to do so... these strange men have chosen to limit the influence and opportunities of women with their distorted interpretation of God's Word.

I turned to the U.F. and said, "not you too, must we always prove a point?" You are doing the same thing we accuse men of doing; you are imposing your views as a standard for women. Hustling unreasonably to prove your strength, is, conforming to another form of slavery and thus a poor standard to judge another woman by. For all you know, she probably has more savings than you. Sincerely, not asking your husband for anything does not make you wiser than a woman who has a husband that takes care of his responsibility; to make money, you leave your kids untended most of the time. And, come home late to still cook and do other house chores with no help from your husband. The sad part is, you can do nothing about it because your husband never listens to you and yet you think you are a good standard? From where I am sitting, I respect you as a woman who is making the best of a bad situation but I do not think that doing your work and your husband's make you a superwoman."

I spoke to her strongly because I was tired of seeing women do to their fellow women what we are telling society to stop doing... I was tired of women shaming other women who choose to be home managers. I was tired of the unnecessary comparison that gets triggered when we see each other as competition; out of envy, we want to act like we are doing better than the other woman. I am tired of young girls sleeping around just because their male counterparts are sleeping around... in their quest to prove a point they forget they are more at risk; men do not get pregnant; men do not do abortions. If a man impregnates a woman and you see him six months later, there is nothing to show you what he did. He would look the same.

I have run out of patience for women who believe fornication or adultery is not a sin when a lady gets no money from it. So, they slut-shame the ones that got an iPhone or a house because they think never getting financial help from your man makes you a champion and a saint.

I prefer to approach gender equality from a point of understanding, it may seem unpopular to some but it's the truth. We should stand for truth, not popular opinion or baseless activism.

Feminism is a fight against stereotypes, a fight for freedom to choose, a fight for justice, a fight against unequal opportunities and a fight against obnoxious boundaries. Not a fight against wisdom, comfort and safety.

#

"And Deborah, a prophetess, the wife of Lapidoth, she judged Israel at that time." Judges 4:4(KJV)

Deborah is a prophetess, a wife and a judge. Wow! Talk about grace, strength and multi-faceted ability.

'She held court under the Palm of Deborah between Ramah and Bethel in the hill country of Ephraim, and the Israelites came to her to have their disputes decided. She sent for Barak son of Abinoam from Kedesh in Naphtali and said to him, "The Lord, the God of Israel, commands you: 'Go, take with you ten thousand men of Naphtali and Zebulun and lead the way to Mount Tabor. I will lure Sisera, the commander of Jabin's army, with his chariots and his troops to the Kishon River and give him into your hands."

Barak said to her, "If you go with me, I will go; but if you don't go with me, I won't go."

"Very well," Deborah said, "I will go with you. But because of the way you are going about this, the honour will not be yours, for the Lord will hand Sisera over to a woman." So Deborah went with Barak to Kedesh, where he summoned Zebulun and

Naphtali. Ten thousand men followed him, and Deborah also went with him. Judg 4:5-10NIV

And they reported to Sisera that Barak the son of Abinoam had gone up to Mount Tabor.So Sisera gathered together all his chariots, nine hundred chariots of iron, and all the people who were with him, from Harosheth Hagoyim to the River Kishon. Then Deborah said to Barak, "Up! For this is the day in which the Lord has delivered Sisera into your hand. Has not the Lord gone out before you?" So Barak went down from Mount Tabor with ten thousand men following him". Judges 4:12-14

Gender can only limit a woman who has not accepted her assignment from God. Did you see that Barak (a man) said he would only go to battle if Deborah (a woman) went with him? When the Lord mobilizes you and you believe in His Grace, your gender is immaterial because no man can deny the anointing upon your life. Barak was a man, but he hearkened to Deborah, the princes of Issachar were with Deborah.1 Chron 12.32 referred to the men of Issachar as men who understood the times and knew what Israel had to do, that the princes of Issachar stood with Deborah is a sign of her strong and effective leadership. It also shows that wise men do not gender-discriminate.

"And the princes of Issachar were with Deborah; even Issachar, and also Barak: he was sent on foot into the valley. For the divisions of Reuben there were great thoughts of heart." Judges 5:15 (KJV)

Deborah was unafraid to fight. She was not afraid to lead. Women in leadership mostly have a harder time exerting authority. Some people hold on to the opinion that women should not lead by citing 1 Tim 2:11-14, that says,

A woman should learn in quietness and full submission. I do not permit a woman to teach or to have authority over a man; she must be silent. For Adam was formed first, then Eve". NIV

And conveniently forget other parts of the bible where women lead or even prophesied. Acts 21:8-10

On the next day we who were Paul's companions departed and came to Caesarea, and entered the house of Philip the evangelist, who was one of the seven, and stayed with him. <u>Now this man had four virgin daughters who prophesied.</u>

One of the key traits of a powerful woman is her willingness to pursue peace and yet have the boldness and strength to make or face a fight, whichever way the Lord leads. Before I realized this, I believed that a woman should only plead, cower, and compromise. I found out later that it doesn't work that way. Being female is not synonymous with being cowardly... you don't always have to run away. Running away every time you face opposition could make your life harder and stop you from fulfilling destiny.

If you have to go to battle for the ones you love, go to battle. Just always ensure that you pray first to make sure that this is the way to handle the situation. Some battles are spiritual- you fight on your knees with the word of God in your mouth and the power of the Holy Spirit. Some are legal, some are intellectual, and some involve standing your ground. Whatever it is, be unafraid if it is for love, honour and righteousness. Go ahead, especially if it's what the Lord has led you to do. Your victory is assured, I congratulate you; I celebrate you. I join you in thanksgiving to our God, who never fails. Hallelujah! The bible says in Judges 5:20 that *"the stars in the courses fought against Sisera"*.

Glory! Heaven's forces are rallied in your favour. Victory is certain.

Jael

"Very well," Deborah said, "I will go with you. But because of the way you are going about this, the honour will not be yours, for the Lord will hand Sisera over to a woman."

Do you remember when Deborah said this to Barak? Well, Jael became that woman who defeated Sisera. She stepped into the prophecy and fulfilled it. When I studied Judges 4:18-24, two things got my attention.

And Jael went out to meet Sisera, and said to him, "Turn aside, my lord, turn aside to me; do not fear." And when he had turned aside with her into the tent, she covered him with a blanket Then he said to her, "Please give me a little water to drink, for I am thirsty." So she opened a jug of milk, gave him a drink, and covered him. And he said to her, "Stand at the door of the tent, and if any man comes and inquires of you, and says, "Is there any man here?" you shall say, 'No."

Then Jael, Heber's wife, took a tent peg and took a hammer in her hand, and went softly to him and drove the peg into his temple, and it went down into the ground; for he was fast asleep and weary. So he died. And then, as Barak pursued Sisera, Jael came out to meet him, and said to him, "Come, I will show you the man whom you seek." And when he went into her tent, there lay Sisera, dead with the peg in his temple.

So on that day God subdued Jabin king of Canaan in the presence of the children of Israel. And the hand of the children of Israel grew stronger and stronger against Jabin king of Canaan, until they had destroyed Jabin king of Canaan. Judges 4:18-24

Jael's strategy was lethal. How could she pull that off?

1   Her understanding: Jael knew this was war and in a war, everyone will eventually have to take sides, so she took sides. Albeit wisely, because when it's war, all that matters is which side you are on.

"Most blessed among women is Jael, The wife of Heber the Kenite; Blessed is she among women in tents. He asked for water, she gave milk; She brought out cream in a lordly bowl. She stretched her hand to the tent peg, Her right hand to the workmen's hammer; She pounded Sisera, she pierced his head, She split and struck through his temple. At her feet he sank, he fell, he lay still; At her feet he sank, he fell where he sank, there he fell dead. Judges 5:24-27. *"*

2   Her pretentious kindness: In a war, the strategies you employ are the next most important things. Here, Jael pretended to be on Sisera's side just to dupe him into trusting her. This made him feel comfortable at her home. I found her actions quite scary- Seriously, who needs enemies when they have friends like Jael. I pray we will not have women like Jael as our enemy. Her actions here show that in a war, the end justifies the means. When righteousness, love, justice, goodness,

freedom and love were at stake, she did what needed to be done.

May we always be courageous. May we always choose wisely; may we choose good over evil, life over death, eternity over momentary, virtues over vices, love over hatred, blessings over curses, grace over damnation.

"Thus let all Your enemies perish, O Lord! But let those who love Him be like the sun when it comes out in full strength. "So the land had rest for forty years". Judges 5:31

Because of Jael's actions, the war ended in victory for the Lord's people with peace in the land.

Jochebed

The name of Amram's wife was Jochebed, a descendant of Levi, who was born to the Levites in Egypt. To Amram she bore Aaron, Moses and their sister Miriam. Num 26:59 NIV

Then Pharaoh gave this order to all his people: "Every boy that is born you must throw into the Nile, but let every girl live." Ex 1:22 NIV

A man from the family of Levi married a Levite woman. The woman became pregnant and had a son. She saw there was something special about him and hid him. She hid him for three months. When she couldn't hide him any longer, she got a little basket-boat made of papyrus, waterproofed it with tar and pitch, and placed the child in it. Then she set it afloat in the reeds at the edge of the Nile. The baby's older sister found herself a vantage point a little way off and watched to see what would happen to him. Pharaoh's daughter came down to the Nile to bathe; her maidens strolled on the bank. She saw the basket-boat floating in the reeds and sent her maid to get it. She opened it and saw the child — a baby crying! Her heart went out to him. She said, "This must be one of the Hebrew babies. Ex 2:1-6 THE MESSAGE

Jochebed was the mother of Moses. She didn't want her son to be killed. So, she strategized to save his life, and she succeeded. She not only saved his life, but she also got to nurse him and she got paid for doing it.

> *Then his sister was before her: "Do you want me to go and get a nursing mother from the Hebrews so she can nurse the baby for you?" Pharaoh's daughter said, "Yes. Go." The girl went and called the child's mother. Pharaoh's daughter told her, "Take this baby and nurse him for me. I'll pay you." The woman took the child and nursed him.* Ex 2:7-9 THE MESSAGE.

Mothers' love is so empowering, Jochebed's love made her take risks... but not recklessly. Did you notice his sister stood at a vantage point observing the basket?

Jochebed must have been an extraordinary woman; she raised the first prophet- Moses, the first high priest, Aaron and the first worship leader, a prophetess - Miriam. Her children were the vessels used by God to free their people from slavery. How remarkable!

Pharoah's Daughter

Then Pharaoh's daughter went down to the Nile to bathe, and her attendants were walking along the river bank. She saw the basket among the reeds and sent her slave girl to get it. She opened it and saw the baby. He was crying, and she felt sorry for him. "This is one of the Hebrew babies," she said.

Then his sister asked Pharaoh's daughter, "Shall I go and get one of the Hebrew women to nurse the baby for you?"

"Yes, go," she answered. And the girl went and got the baby's mother. Pharaoh's daughter said to her, "Take this baby and nurse him for me, and I will pay you." So the woman took the baby and nursed him. When the child grew older, she took him to Pharaoh's daughter, and he became her son. She named him Moses, saying, "I drew him out of the water." Ex 2:5-10NIV.

All mothers are amazing, birth mothers are great, but I particularly want to celebrate mothers-by-adoption because they don't have the advantage of pregnancy-induced-nurture hormones. Nature did not thrust motherhood on them. Rather, foster or adoptive parents are such rare gems because they choose to love and care for children birthed by others. Every splendid mother has a high level of the capacity to love, but raising another woman's child takes an even higher degree of the capacity to love.

Pharaoh's daughter fell in love and was determined to care for a child that was not hers, a child that belonged to a people whom her father wanted dead. She chose to protect that child and treat him like her own. It is commendable; I don't think it would have been a light thing for her to adopt a Hebrew child and raise him in the palace! Especially after her father had already decreed to have them killed.

Many people still struggle with accepting other kids- being step-parents, legal guardians or foster parents. I pray they learn a thing or two from Pharaoh's daughter; love has no barrier. It does not recognise colour, tribe, language or laws. Love seeks to preserve, give, care and protect.

Rahab

Sometimes people wander into prostitution because life's challenges left them little or no choice. But they don't have to stay there. There is a way out. Will they embrace it? Are they ready to do things differently?

> *Likewise also was not Rahab the harlot justified by works, when she had received the messengers, and had sent them out another way? For as the body without the spirit is dead, so faith without works is dead also.* James 2:25-26

In the birth genealogy of our Lord Jesus, *Salmon begot Boaz by Rahab, Boaz begot Obed by Ruth, Obed begot Jesse, and Jesse begot David the king.* Matt 1:5-6.

We read that Rahab married Salmon and became the mother of Boaz, who was the grand-dad of David... amazing, God will not consult your past to bless you. All you have to do is repent and trust Him.

> *By faith the harlot Rahab perished not with them that believed not, when she had received the spies with peace.* Heb 11:31

> *"Now Joshua the son of Nun sent out two men from Acacia Grove to spy secretly, saying, "Go, view the land, especially*

Jericho." So they went, and came to the house of a harlot named Rahab, and lodged there. And it was told the king of Jericho, saying, "Behold, men have come here tonight from the children of Israel to search out the country." So the king of Jericho sent to Rahab, saying, "Bring out the men who have come to you, who have entered your house, for they have come to search out all the country."

Then the woman took the two men and hid them. So she said, "Yes, the men came to me, but I did not know where they were from. And it happened as the gate was being shut, when it was dark, that the men went out. Where the men went I do not know; pursue them quickly, for you may overtake them."(But she had brought them up to the roof and hidden them with the stalks of flax, which she had laid in order on the roof.) Then the men pursued them by the road to the Jordan, to the fords. And as soon as those who pursued them had gone out, they shut the gate.

Now before they lay down, she came up to them on the roof, and said to the men:" I know that the Lord has given you the land, that the terror of you has fallen on us, and that all the inhabitants of the land are fainthearted because of you.

For we have heard how the Lord dried up the water of the Red Sea for you when you came out of Egypt, and what you did to the two kings of the Amorites who were on the other side of the Jordan, Sihon and Og, whom you utterly destroyed. And as soon as we heard these things, our hearts melted; neither did there remain any more courage in anyone because of you, for the Lord your God, He is God in heaven above and on earth beneath. Now therefore, I beg you, swear to me by the Lord, since I have shown you kindness, that you also will show kindness to my father's house, and give me a true token, and spare my father, my mother, my brothers, my sisters, and all that they have, and deliver our lives from death."

So the men answered her, "Our lives for yours, if none of you tell this business of ours. And it shall be, when the Lord has given us the land, that we will deal kindly and truly with you."

Then she let them down by a rope through the window, for her house was on the city wall; she dwelt on the wall. And she said to them, "Get to the mountain, lest the pursuers meet you. Hide there for three days, until the pursuers have returned. Afterwards you may go your way." So the men said to her: "We will be blameless of this oath of yours which you have made us swear, unless, when we come into the land, you bind this line of scarlet cord in the window through which you let us down, and unless you bring your father, your mother, your brothers, and all your father's household to your own home. So it shall be that whoever goes outside the doors of your house into the street, his blood shall be on his own head, and we will be guiltless. And whoever is with you in the house, his blood shall be on our head if a hand is laid on him. And if you tell this business of ours, then we will be free from your oath which you made us swear."

Then she said, "According to your words, so be it." And she sent them away, and they departed. And she bound the scarlet cord in the window. They departed and went to the mountain, and stayed there three days until the pursuers returned. The pursuers sought them all along the way, but did not find them. So the two men returned, descended from the mountain, and crossed over; and they came to Joshua the son of Nun, and told him all that had befallen them. And they said to Joshua, "Truly the Lord has delivered all the land into our hands, for indeed all the inhabitants of the country are fainthearted because of us." Josh 2:1-24

Rahab was the woman who proved that once a prostitute, does not always mean a prostitute. Rahab negotiated her way out of shame to glory.

Rahab took the right side and earned herself a second chance at a new life and protection for her family. She was helpful to the right side. Every day in this life, we make choices that can either make us or mar us.

Rahab observed that the people were afraid of the Israelites. Rahab knew there was going to be a war and, in every war, the God side is the winning side. It doesn't matter who agrees or disagrees.

The winning side could mean feeding the hungry, helping the destitute, lifting the downtrodden, accepting salvation in Jesus Christ, telling someone about the gospel, serving God faithfully, protecting the rights of the less privileged, praying for someone, speaking a word of grace, buying this book for more women and loving and honouring God through your lifestyles... Always choose the winning side.

The Midwives

The king of Egypt spoke to the Hebrew midwives, of whom the name of the one was Shiphrah, and the name of the other Puah, and he said, "When you perform the duty of a midwife to the Hebrew women, and see them on the birth stool; if it is a son, then you shall kill him; but if it is a daughter, then she shall live." But the midwives feared God, and didn't do what the king of Egypt commanded them, but saved the baby boys alive. The king of Egypt called for the midwives, and said to them, "Why have you done this thing, and have saved the boys alive?"

The midwives said to Pharaoh, "Because the Hebrew women aren't like the Egyptian women; for they are vigorous, and give birth before the midwife comes to them."

God dealt well with the midwives, and the people multiplied, and grew very mighty. It happened, because the midwives feared God, that he gave them families. Ex 1:15-21 WEB.

These women were preservers of destiny and their good deeds didn't go unrewarded. This encourages us to do good for humanity and try to save lives wherever we find ourselves because God sees everything; He hates wickedness and the shedding of blood.

The midwives could have worked with Pharaoh in doing evil and said, "It's not our responsibility, we are just following orders," and by inaction, they would have been accomplices to murder. But, no, they were wiser because they had the fear of the Lord in their hearts. Do you have the fear of the Lord? It helps us live our lives more conscientiously. There are repercussions for mean actions and rewards for kind deeds. Even when we think nobody knows, there is an invisible camera following us every day.

The Daughters of Reuel

Now the priest of Midian had seven daughters. And they came and drew water, and they filled the troughs to water their father's flock. Then the shepherds came and drove them away, <u>but Moses stood up and helped them</u> and watered their flock. When they came to Reuel their father, he said, "<u>How is it that you have come so soon today?</u>"

And they said, "An Egyptian delivered us from the hand of the shepherds, and he also drew enough water for us and watered the flock." Ex 2:16-19 NKJV

What does being called a wise and strong woman mean?

How do we define wisdom and strength? Wisdom is the ability to know what needs to be done. Strength is the ability to do what needs to be done. Sometimes, strength means accepting help.

I saw a picture of a stranded woman, somewhere. The caption said that she was a feminist who had refused to join the children of Israel when they were crossing the red sea because she insisted on using her own rod to part the red sea. Even under such dire circumstances, she allegedly refused to change her policy which stated that it was wrong to accept help from a man. While I was laughing so hard, someone interrupted me and said, there are women who are that obstinate. Are there?

Just like we read in the scripture above, the daughters of Reuel were being intimidated, but then came Moses (the knight in shining armour) and helped them out. Some men like to cheat and look down on women. Such men like to make things harder for them. They want to deny them their right to live, be accomplished, happy and self-sufficient. But not all men are like that; some men are powerful advocates for women's rights. A lot of men are helpful and kind. It would be unwise to brand all men as abusive because of the actions of some insecure, mean-spirited fellows.

Did you realise that Reuel, their father, was surprised that they came back earlier? Dear woman, learn to accept help whenever it is genuinely offered because receiving help does not undermine you. Don't cheat yourself or obstinately make things cumbersome. Rather, make your life easier by using available resources to make your work faster. There are still good men out there. Pray for the gift of good men; men that can help you without ulterior motives. Pray that God will send them your way and you will have the ability to recognise them. Be wise, not every relationship is about sexual favours or dominance.

The Syrophoenician Woman

A lesson on persistence.

From there He arose and went to the region of Tyre and Sidon. And He entered a house and wanted no one to know it, but He could not be hidden. For a woman whose young daughter had an unclean spirit heard about Him, and she came and fell at His feet. The woman was a Greek, a Syro-Phoenician by birth, and she kept asking Him to cast the demon out of her daughter. But Jesus said to her, "Let the children be filled first, for it is not good to take the children's bread and throw it to the little dogs." And she answered and said to Him, "Yes, Lord, yet even the little dogs under the table eat from the children's crumbs."

Then He said to her, "For this saying go your way; the demon has gone out of your daughter." And when she had come to her house, she found the demon gone out, and her daughter lying on the bed. Mark 7:24-30

Sometimes we miss our blessings because of impatience and anger. Truth is, we are special to God, but we must never forget that God doesn't exist because of us. Rather, we exist because of

God. Understanding that God will be God, irrespective of our acknowledgement, will help us stay humble and get all the blessings we require. The Syrophoenician woman understood this, and that is why she could get what she wanted. She could have lost faith. She could have gotten angry when the Lord implied she was not a - priority or she was not qualified or she needed to wait - by saying let the children be fed first because it is not good to take the children's bread and give it to little dogs. I can just imagine some people rudely interrupting the Lord and asking, "Who are you referring to as a little dog, just because I need a favour from you?" But not the Syro-Phoenician women, she was too wise for that. She said, *"Yes, Lord, yet even the little dogs under the table eat from the children's crumbs"*. A wise, humble woman, no wonder the Lord said, *"For this saying go your way; the demon has gone out of your daughter"*. Hallelujah!

Do not lose faith. Learn to be persistent because when we diligently and humbly seek God's intervention, we will get it. Jesus told them a story showing that it was necessary for them to pray consistently and never quit. He said, *"There was once a judge in some city who never gave God a thought and cared nothing for people. A widow in that city kept after him: 'My rights are being violated. Protect me!' "He never gave her the time of day. But after this went on and on he said to himself, 'I care nothing what God thinks, even less what people think. But because this widow won't quit badgering me, I'd better do something and see that she gets justice — otherwise I'm going to end up beaten black and blue by her pounding." Then the Master said, "Do you hear what that judge, corrupt as he is, is saying? So what makes you think God won't step in and work justice for his chosen people, who continue to cry out for help? Won't he stick up for them? I assure you, he will. He will not drag his feet. But how much of that kind of persistent faith will the Son of Man find on the earth when he returns?"* Luke 18:1-8

The Elect Lady

From the elder, to an elect lady and her children, whom I love in truth (and not I alone, but also all those who know the truth), because of the truth that resides in us and will be with us forever. Grace, mercy, and peace will be with us from God the Father and from Jesus Christ the Son of the Father, in truth and love.

I rejoiced greatly because I have found some of your <u>children living according to the truth</u>, just as the Father commanded us. But now I ask you, lady (not as if I were writing a new commandment to you, but the one we have had from the beginning), <u>that we love one another</u>. (Now this is love: that we walk according to his commandments.) This is the commandment, just as you have heard from the beginning; thus you should walk in it.   <u>For many deceivers have gone out</u> into the world, people who do not confess Jesus as Christ coming in the flesh. This person is the deceiver and the antichrist<u>!   Watch out, so that you do not lose the things we have worked for, but receive a full reward.</u>

Everyone who goes on ahead and does not remain in the teaching of Christ does not have God. The one who remains in this teaching has both the Father and the Son. <u>If anyone comes to you and does not bring this teaching, do not receive him into</u>

your house and do not give him any greeting, because the person who gives him a greeting shares in his evil deeds. Though I have many other things to write to you, I do not want to do so with paper and ink, but I hope to come visit you and speak face to face, so that our joy may be complete. The children of your elect sister greet you. 2 John The NET Bible

Who is an elect lady? She is a beloved, special and respected lady who has distinguished herself through her good works. Also, from the scriptures, we read that she has raised godly children.

Despite being a Christian, she is being reminded to remain in truth; to keep living a life inspired by love because all our good works are meaningless if genuine love does not motivate them.

Sometimes, our accomplishments can make us think we are infallible. They can make us accrue superpowers we do not possess to ourselves. Thus, making us arrogant and negligent. The elect lady is told to be careful because there are many deceivers in the world; eloquent liars who play down what is really important, antichrists disguised as followers of Christ. She is also informed on how to tell the fakes from the original - the fakes deny that Jesus Christ came in an actual body.

She is reminded of the danger of falling for their lies - falling for their lies could mean losing the reward she has worked so hard for. So, be careful where you sow your seeds... don't just support everything because they pretend to be Christians. This passage reminds me again of the scripture that says, *"Beloved, believe not every spirit, but try the spirits whether they are of God: because many false prophets are gone out into the world. Hereby know ye the Spirit of God: Every spirit that confesseth that Jesus Christ is come in the flesh is of God: And every spirit that confesseth not that Jesus Christ is come in the flesh is not of God: and this is that spirit of antichrist, whereof ye have heard that it should come; and even now already is it in the world. Ye are of God, little children, and have overcome them: because greater is he that is in you, than he that is in the world".* 1 John 4:1-4.

Mary Magdalene

"And it came to pass afterwards, that he went throughout every city and village, preaching and showing the glad tidings of the kingdom of God: and the twelve were with him, And certain women, which had been healed of evil spirits and infirmities, Mary called Magdalene, out of whom went seven devils, And Joanna the wife of Chuza Herod's steward, and Susanna, and many others, which ministered unto him of their substance." Luke 8:1-3

Mary Magdalene indicates how a person's life can change once she accepts Christ. Her story shows that who you were is insubstantial once God steps in; your past is immaterial in view of your future in Christ.

Look at this, she was described as the woman **"out of whom went out seven demons"** what a description. What kind of life would she have had without Jesus Christ? Thank God for Jesus! Demons are synonymous with evil, sin, uncleanliness, baggage and unpleasantness. Yet, she didn't allow the stigma of such a past to stop her from serving God. See, now that you are born again, nothing should hold you back from going all out for Jesus and living a good life.

Remember, "Old things are passed away. Behold, all things have become new... He that the Son set free is free indeed." So, become a participator in the divine experience.

You don't have to have a perfect past to serve God. Mary Magdalene was among the women who partnered with the Lord by ministering unto Him from their resources. Mary Magdalene let her life count for good despite what the enemy had planned. It is often said that the gospel is free but not cheap because organising crusades, being on TV, going for evangelical missions, printing books etc, cost a lot of money. Every time you enjoy a free meal in church or get a free counselling session, someone is going to pay or has given to make it possible.

We can do a lot better if everyone realises that pastors pay bills too. There was a time when I cried out to God because I spent hours talking to people for free and I didn't yet have partners sponsoring the work. I almost backslid under the financial pressure I was under. Thank God for kind people. Women who supported God's work out of their own means, like Joana, Susanna and Mary Magdalene, are the real MVPs.

Martha (The Sister Of Mary And Lazarus)

"Now it came to pass, as they went, that he entered into a certain village: and a certain woman named Martha received him into her house. And she had a sister called Mary, which also sat at Jesus' feet, and heard his word. But Martha was cumbered about much serving, and came to him, and said, Lord, dost thou not care that my sister hath left me to serve alone? bid her therefore that she help me. Luke 10: 38-40

And Jesus answered and said to her, "Martha, Martha, you are worried and troubled about many things. But one thing is needed, and Mary has chosen that good part, which will not be taken away from her." Luke 10:41-42

Have you ever found yourself perturbed about the number of things you have to do?

Have you ever wished you had more workers or tools or help?

Have you ever felt like you have a deadline to meet, there isn't enough time and yet no one seems to care?

Have you ever wondered if you have what it takes to win?

If your answer is yes, then you probably feel like Martha; with a distinguished, honourable, stately, anointed guest like Jesus, and not enough hands to help showcase your hospitality and prove your culinary expertise. You probably felt, Mary, your sister was your enemy for not supporting your desire to be the perfect hostess.

The thing with being stressed is that it stops you from seeing that things do not have to be complicated; it makes you think everyone is unhelpful. It makes you feel like everyone else is wrong and you are the only one doing what needs to be done.

Martha was doing the right thing at the wrong time. She lacked the revelation of who Jesus is and so related to Him like a normal man. Typically, whenever we are in an-everything-depends-on-me-mood, we lose sight of important details.

With Jesus, the important thing was not food, but fellowship. God is not interested in fruitless activities that keep us away from Him.

Martha was a special case. To think she went to report Mary to Jesus and asked Him to instruct her to come and lend her a hand tells us more about the character of Martha. She sure seemed presumptuous. The Lord's response made me excited; He knows us more than we know ourselves. Jesus said, "... you are fussing far too much and getting yourself worked up over nothing."

In your walk with God, never substitute activities for fellowship. All that matters is staying connected to God, relishing your relationship, basking in His presence through worship and study of His word. I always tell my brethren that if I have too much to do and have to leave out one. I ensure it's never anything that has to do with God.

The ministry of the Holy Spirit is so important; we must never forget it is from the presence of God that we get the grace and strength to accomplish other tasks. No matter how busy you are, always create time for God because He is the giver of time and ability.

Have you ever asked someone to eat on your behalf? Who has ever said, "Bob I'm so hungry but I must handle this project so kindly eat for me." No! Even the busiest man cannot delegate eating. Eating is something you must create time for and do by yourself, because you can only enjoy the benefit when you do it yourself. Fellowshiping with God is like that. It is an absolute necessity, so let's not prioritise wrongly.

One thing is needed, never forget ... seek first the kingdom and everything else will be added unto you.

Rebekah

"And it came to pass, before he had done speaking, that, behold, Rebekah came out, who was born to Bethuel, son of Milcah, the wife of Nahor, Abraham's brother, with her pitcher upon her shoulder. And the damsel was very fair to look upon, a virgin, neither had any man known her: and she went down to the well, and filled her pitcher, and came up. And the servant ran to meet her, and said, Let me, I pray thee, drink a little water of thy pitcher. And she said, Drink, my lord: and she hasted, and let down her pitcher upon her hand, and gave him drink." Gen 24:15-18

"Well, when I came this very day to the spring, I prayed, 'God, God of my master Abraham, make things turn out well in this task I've been given. I'm standing at this well. When a young woman comes here to draw water and I say to her, Please, give me a sip of water from your jug, and she says, Not only will I give you a drink, I'll also water your camels — let that woman be the wife God has picked out for my master's son.' "I had barely finished offering this prayer, when Rebekah arrived, her jug on her shoulder. She went to the spring and drew water and I said, 'Please, can I have a drink?' She didn't hesitate. She held out her jug and said, 'Drink; and when you're finished I'll also water your camels.' I drank, and she watered the camels. I asked her, 'Whose daughter are you?' She said, 'The daughter of Bethuel whose parents were Nahor and Milcah.' I gave her a ring for her nose, bracelets for her arms, Gen 24:42-48 MSG

Our predisposed or default attitude always influences the quality of our lives. Rebecca passed the kindness test even though she didn't know she was being tested because she is naturally a helpful person.

Dear single lady, dear married wife, hear this- **kindness makes you attractive.** Kindness is an attribute that shows you are godly. Kindness makes you an answer to someone's prayer. Also, kindness helps you soar in the business place. Too many people want to be accepted the way they are; they think their mean streak, insensitivity and lack of empathetic reasoning should not affect their relationships. This is an error. Kindness opens a door of interest through which we build meaningful relationships.

If Rebecca had refused to help the stranger, she would have missed that divine opportunity, and the sad part is unkind people hardly know what blessings pass them by, they don't know what they've missed.

Now I am not saying that you should talk to every Tom, Dick and Harry. I am not saying you should cook for everyone and be a friend with benefits to everyone who shows an interest. No, a lady must learn how to maintain boundaries without being uppity and mean; you should understand the terms of any relationship before going in.

I am saying be good, be kind, without taking leave of your senses. I am saying to be helpful because the world would be a better place if we all practice kindness.

Even though kindness releases blessings and brings promotions, let it flow naturally; you don't have to desperately go searching... trying to prove you are kind. Kindness is unassuming, we express it in the little things. My husband said when he met me, he wondered how I could be so warm and smile so much until we got to know each other better, then he understood the concept of default setting. He fell in love with my default setting. My default setting is to smile, listen, and be helpful. Anytime I acted differently, I felt uncomfortable and automatically reverted to it.

I heard about a young lady who went to visit her boyfriend's family and pretended to be a goody-two-shoes. She warmed her way into the heart of every member of the family so much that they insisted their son marry her immediately. After the wedding, she became not just nonchalant about their needs, feelings, and the good relationship they thought they had. She became a devil. She met her Waterloo when she started disrespecting her husband and starving her maid for days. A neighbour who witnessed her unkindness towards her maid reported her to a human rights organisation. And she was arrested for crimes against humanity. After that incident, her husband ousted her out of her position with little ado.

Why do people pretend! If you can act kind, then be kind. Pretending to be kind just because of the results is hypocritical. It defeats the beauty of pure goodness. Being kind is easier than acting kind. It is so invigorating.

Rebekah is quite something, see

After Isaac had become old and almost blind, he called in his first-born son Esau, who asked him, "Father, what can I do for you?" Isaac replied, "I am old and might die at any time. So take your bow and arrows, then go out in the fields, and kill a wild animal. Cook some of that tasty food that I love so much and bring it to me. I want to eat it once more and give you my blessing before I die."

Rebekah had been <u>listening, and as soon as Esau left to go hunting, she said to Jacob, "I heard your father tell Esau to kill a wild animal and cook some tasty food for your father before he dies. Your father said this because he wants to bless your brother with the Lord as his witness. Now, my son, listen carefully to what I want you to do.</u> Go and kill two of your best young goats and bring them to me. I'll cook the tasty food that your father loves so much. <u>Then you can take it to him, so he can eat it and give you his blessing before he dies.</u>

<u>"My brother Esau is a hairy man," Jacob reminded her. "And I am not. If my father touches me and realizes I am trying to trick him, he will put a curse on me instead of giving me a blessing." Rebekah insisted, "Let his curse fall on me! Just do what I say and bring me the meat."</u> So Jacob brought the meat to his mother, and she cooked the tasty food that his father liked. Then she took Esau's best clothes and put them on Jacob. She also covered the smooth part of his hands and neck with goatskins and gave him some bread and the tasty food she had cooked. Jacob went to his father and said, "Father, here I am." "Which one of my sons are you?" his father asked. Jacob replied, "I am Esau, your first-born, and I have done what you told me. Please sit up and eat the meat I have brought. Then you can give me your

blessing." Isaac asked, "My son, how did you find an animal so quickly?"

"The Lord your God was kind to me," Jacob answered. "My son," Isaac said, "come closer, where I can touch you and find out if you really are Esau." Jacob went clo

ser. His father touched him and said, "You sound like Jacob, but your hands feel hairy like Esau's." And so Isaac blessed Jacob, thinking he was Esau. Gen 27:15-23 CEV.

Why did Rebecca help her son defraud his brother?

After all, they are both her children. Didn't she know it could ruin their relationship?

Perhaps it was because she disapproved of Esau's choice of wife? But that seemed like an excuse to make Isaac ask Jacob to go to her family. Read.

When Rebekah found out what Esau planned to do, she sent for Jacob and told him, "Son, your brother Esau is just waiting for the time when he can kill you. Now listen carefully and do what I say. Go to the home of my brother Laban in Haran and stay with him for a while. When Esau stops being angry and forgets what you have done to him, I'll send for you to come home. Why should I lose both of my sons on the same day?" Rebekah later told Isaac, "Those Hittite wives of Esau are making my life miserable! If Jacob marries a Hittite woman, I'd be better off dead."

Isaac called in Jacob, then gave him a blessing, and said: Don't marry any of those Canaanite women. Go at once to your mother's father Bethuel in northern Syria and choose a wife from one of the daughters of Laban, your mother's brother. Gen 27:42-28:2 CEV.

Rebekah proved how influential women can be; she already decided Jacob should go to Laban and just had to subtly introduce the thought to her husband Isaac.

She was quite a strategist; her actions couldn't have been influenced by just favouritism, possibly because she loved both her sons. She lamented about not losing them both and ensured they stayed in different cities to preserve their lives.

 What she did was so dangerous. Jacob was afraid to go through with it; deceiving his father was no light feat. But instead of Rebekah stopping her conniving, she staked her life. There are some questions about Rebekah that we can never really answer. But I view her as a matriarch whose actions probably saved an entire nation. Since they were her children, she knew them better and knew Jacob was more deserving of the blessing. Perhaps Esau, who the bible defined as profane, may have traded it to a stranger.

Vashti

Vashti was the woman who lost her crown because of pride.

Many people are familiar with the story of queen Esther, but very few know about queen Vashti even though Vashti was Esther's predecessor. It was Vashti's error that produced queen Esther; if Vashti had not publicly disdained her husband, king Xerxes, she would not have been replaced by Esther.

This is the story of something that happened in the time of Xerxes, the Xerxes who ruled from India to Ethiopia — 127 provinces in all. King Xerxes ruled from his royal throne in the palace complex of Susa. In the third year of his reign he gave a banquet for all his officials and ministers. The military brass of Persia and Media were also there, along with the princes and governors of the provinces. For six months he put on exhibit the huge wealth of his empire and its stunningly beautiful royal splendours. At the conclusion of the exhibit, the king threw a weeklong party for everyone living in Susa, the capital — important and unimportant alike. The party was in the garden courtyard of the king's summer house. The courtyard was elaborately decorated with white and blue cotton curtains tied with linen and purple cords to silver rings on marble columns. Silver and gold couches were arranged on a mosaic pavement of porphyry, marble, mother-of-

pearl, and coloured stones. Drinks were served in gold chalices, each chalice one-of-a-kind. The royal wine flowed freely — a generous king!

The guests could drink as much as they liked — king's orders! — with waiters at their elbows to refill the drinks. Meanwhile, Queen Vashti was throwing a separate party for women inside King Xerxes' royal palace. On the seventh day of the party, the king, high on the wine, ordered the seven eunuchs who were his personal servants (Mehuman, Biztha, Harbona, Bigtha, Abagtha, Zethar, and Carcas) to bring him Queen Vashti resplendent in her royal crown. He wanted to show off her beauty to the guests and officials. She was extremely good-looking. But Queen Vashti refused to come, refused the summons delivered by the eunuchs. The king lost his temper. Seething with anger over her insolence, the king called in his counsellors, all experts in legal matters. It was the king's practice to consult his expert advisors. Those closest to him were Carshena, Shethar, Admatha, Tarshish, Meres, Marsena, and Memucan, the seven highest-ranking princes of Persia and Media, the inner circle with access to the king's ear. He asked them what legal recourse they had against Queen Vashti for not obeying King Xerxes' summons delivered by the eunuchs. Memucan spoke up in the council of the king and princes: "It's not only the king Queen Vashti has insulted; it's all of us, leaders and people alike in every last one of King Xerxes' provinces. The word's going to get out: 'Did you hear the latest about Queen Vashti? King Xerxes ordered her to be brought before him and she wouldn't do it!' When the women hear it, they'll start treating their husbands with contempt. The day the wives of the Persian and Mede officials get wind of the queen's insolence, they'll be out of control. Is that what we want, a country of angry women who don't know their place?

"So, if the king agrees, let him pronounce a royal ruling and have it recorded in the laws of the Persians and Medes so that it cannot be revoked, that Vashti is permanently banned from King Xerxes' presence. And then let the king give her royal position to a woman who knows her place. When the king's ruling becomes public knowledge throughout the kingdom, extensive as it is, every woman, regardless of her social position, will show proper respect to her husband." Est 1:1-20MSB

As a child of God, your King is first, God, God is everything. Never forget that without His Grace you won't exist. God has made you all you are. Honouring him with your life is such a small price to pay. Worshipping God with a heart of gratitude and humility is so empowering and refreshing.

Vashti forgot she was only a queen because of the king. Some people easily besmirch those who elevated them; what brand of stupidity is that? Vashti was not born a queen; she got a crown only because she got the king. Sadly, she got carried away with being queen and forgot about honouring her king, serving him and attending to his needs.

Never let familiarity rob you of the ability to be reverent to your king; some women can be respectful to every man but not their husbands.

Here is a simple secret. As women, one thing we must learn to do is to choose our battles wisely because not everything is worth a fight. We must not have a differing opinion just for the sake of it. Strength of character is not expressed by being difficult or combatant. Rather, true strength is to be wisely discerning, knowing when to give in and when to insist.

The place of a woman is delicate yet powerful. You must know your position so you can occupy it beautifully. When you understand the power you wield, you will not get unduly defensive when you are told to stay in your place. Enlightened women hardly get offended when they are referred to as mere women because they know there is nothing mere, casual, derogatory, inferior, shameful, or ordinary about being a woman. So, rather than pick a fight, they take advantage of the extra power they can wield from being under-estimated.

Wisdom can help you caution yourself whenever you want to overreact or be overly defensive over the demands and expectations being a woman entails. Patience will help you not exert your energy in trying to prove you are sufficient to unlearned folks who are still living in denial - ignorant of the magnificent masterpiece called woman.

The king, Vashti's husband, asked his officials to bring his queen, Vashti, but she refused to come. Was his demand obnoxious? Was his expectation presumptuous? Look at this. Let us consider what could have made Queen Vashti respond the way she did?

Perhaps she was probably one of those women who are fond of reasoning defensively. They ask questions like these and draw the wrong conclusions:

Why should I cook?

Why should I ask my husband for his opinion before I get my hair cut?

Why should I attend this event, am I a trophy to be displayed?

Why should I take permission from my husband before I travel?

Why should I tell my husband before having a nose job, or abortion or liposuction?

Truth is, they are right and they are wrong too because being a wife does not mean losing your identity. It does not mean losing your voice or the ability to decide for yourself.

Being a wife means recognising that you are not solely in charge of your life anymore. It means you are not the only stakeholder in your life anymore, thus, every decision affects the other stakeholders. Being a wife means you probably have someone who cares as much about you as you do about yourself. Being a wife means talking to your husband, listening to his opinions, tendering your submissions or inhibitions with humility, love and wisdom, and deferring to him willingly by choice.

Women sometimes have an issue submitting to their husbands for either of these reasons.

> **They are too independent:** In this case; you must discuss your views on remaining unyielding with your future husband and marry someone with similar views to avoid heartbreak. You could also choose to remain unmarried; marriage is not for everyone. Marriage

involves the two parties depending on each other, giving and accepting support, with the man as the head and the woman submitting to him.

They don't trust their husband: If you are not yet married, I must tell you that this is very important; do not marry a man you do not trust. When some men demand submission, they do not care if they have earned your trust. Some people don't care if they lead correctly or not, they just want you to follow. So, if you don't trust his love, you won't trust his motives. If you don't trust his intentions, you cannot trust his direction; a part of you will resist his instructions and leadership. He will fight back. So, if you are not yet married, take counsel, think thrice before marrying a man you do not trust. There is no quick solution to remedy such an error because it is a foundational problem. It mostly ends in a painful vicious cycle; where the man will resent the woman for not giving in to his leadership. If you are married and you are experiencing this - difficulty trusting and yielding to your husband's authority, please consider counselling. Foundational problems can be managed, but it requires a lot of determination, knowledge, prayers and patience.

Vashti lived through the scriptural consequences of pride, "First pride, then the crash — the bigger the ego, the harder the fall." *Prov 16:18 MSB.*

"When pride comes, then comes shame; but with the humble is wisdom." *Prov 11:2.*

"A man's pride shall bring him low: but honour shall uphold the humble in spirit." *Prov. 29:23.*

If Queen Vashti had learnt about honour, wisdom would have propelled her to act differently. Considering her husband's position, what she did seemed like a smear campaign. An honourable king should not be treated with disdain publicly by his wife! This goes to show that inappropriate behaviour cannot be hidden for too long. If you disrespect your husband in your heart and in your home, before long you will do it publicly without knowing. Honour starts from the heart, free from prying eyes and majorly influenced by our perception... but it eventually affects our attitude and everything else.

Since Vashti was a role model to the women of Persia, you would have expected her to know that her husband's desire to showcase her beauty is something she should be happy about and not be on the defensive for. Come on! A wise woman lets her king brag with her. It is a blessing. Vashti probably didn't know she was dethroning herself when she dishonoured her husband and chose the path of obstinacy in front of the entire kingdom, but that cut deeply and she paid dearly because ignorance was not a defence.

Pick your battles wisely; I can't stress this enough because it is one of the key lessons from Vashti's life. Before you resist your husband, ask yourself these questions:

- What am I being asked to do?
- Is what he is suggesting a bad thing?
- Is it going to hurt me or others?

- Why am I not happy about this? (Sometimes it's just hormones. Sometimes it is not and you are right)
- Who is watching?
- Could I have misunderstood?
- Is there a preconceived misconception?
- Do I have to resist (sometimes the answer is yes)?
- What is the best way to express my disagreement or displeasure?
- How do I resist effectively?
- What is at stake?

As much as you may prefer to accept every decision your spouse makes, there may be times when that decision may not be in the best interest of your family. If they base the decision on an error of judgement and you feel you have to resist – do it the right way; always pray about everything and communicate in love.

Esther

After a while, King Xerxes got over being angry. But he kept thinking about what Vashti had done and the law that he had written because of her. Then the king's personal servants said: Your Majesty, a search must be made to find you some beautiful young women. You can select officers in every province to bring them to the place where you keep your wives in the capital city of Susa. Put your servant Hegai in charge of them since that is his job. He can see to it that they are given the proper beauty treatments. Then let the young woman who pleases you most take Vashti's place as queen. King Xerxes liked these suggestions, and he followed them. At this time a Jew named Mordecai was living in Susa. His father was Jair, and his grandfather Shimei was the son of Kish from the tribe of Benjamin. Kish was one of the people that Nebuchadnezzar had taken from Jerusalem, when he took King Jeconiah of Judah to Babylonia. Est 2:1-6 CEV.

Mordecai had a cousin named Hadassah, whom he had brought up because she had neither father nor mother. This girl, who was also known as Esther, was lovely in form and features, and Mordecai had taken her as his own daughter when her father and mother died. When the king's order and edict had been proclaimed, many girls were brought to the citadel of Susa and put under the care of Hegai. Esther also was taken to the king's palace and entrusted to Hegai, who had charge of the harem. The girl pleased him and won his *favour. Immediately he provided her with her beauty treatments and special food. He assigned to her seven maids selected from the king's palace and moved her and her maids into the best place in the harem.* Esther had not revealed her nationality and family background, because Mordecai had forbidden her to do so. Every day he walked back and forth near the courtyard of the harem to find out how Esther was and what was happening to her. *Before a girl's turn came to go in to King Xerxes, she had to complete twelve months of beauty treatments prescribed for the women, six months with oil of myrrh and six with perfumes and cosmetics.* And this is how she would go to the king: Anything she wanted was given her to take with her from the harem to the king's palace. In the evening she would go there and in the morning return to another part of the harem to the care of Shaashgaz, the king's eunuch who was in charge of the concubines. She would not return to the king unless he was pleased with her and summoned her by name. When the turn came for Esther (the girl Mordecai had adopted, the daughter of his uncle Abihail) to go to the king, she asked for nothing other than what Hegai, the king's eunuch who was in charge of the harem, suggested. And Esther won the favour of everyone who saw her. She was taken to King Xerxes in the royal residence in the tenth month, the month of Tebeth, in the seventh year of his reign. Now the king was attracted to Esther more than to any of the other women, and she won his favour and approval more than any of the other virgins. So he set a royal crown on her head and made her queen instead of Vashti. And the king gave a great banquet, Esther's banquet, for all his nobles and officials. He proclaimed a holiday throughout the provinces and distributed gifts with royal liberality. Esth 2:7-18 NIV.*

Beautiful, favoured and humble. Esther was an orphan, but she had a father figure, her uncle, who deemed it fit to enrol her for the contest. Once in the contest, grace took over and Esther found favour. Esther was preferred above others. We cannot say if Esther did anything special to earn this favour but we know she did nothing wrong either. *"When the turn came for Esther (the girl Mordecai had adopted, the daughter of his uncle Abihail) to go to the king, <u>she asked for nothing other than what Hegai, the king's eunuch who was in charge of the harem, suggested</u>. And Esther won the favour of everyone who saw her."* We know from this scripture that she was not greedy or presumptuous or overbearing or demanding or disrespectful. In the real scheme of things, an excellent character speaks louder than looks and is the perfect embellishment of a beautiful face.

The gift of love and acceptance is by grace, yes; love cannot always be earned, but having excellent character, humility and confidence is an enormous advantage when seeking favour as these are always considered when judging the beauty, appeal, quality and comeliness of a woman.

Did you notice they made Esther queen even though nothing was known about her family and past? This shows that when grace and wisdom are at work, you can become anybody. There is no limit to how high you can rise; you can be as great as you want despite your background.

Esther was counselled to be discreet, and she was discreet until the appointed time. I heard about a young lady who was heartbroken because she felt she told her boyfriend too much about herself. After telling him how many men she had been with and how dysfunctional her family was, he started mistreating her. He used the information she had given him to emotionally abuse her. The relationship eventually packed up. She felt terrible because before she told him so much about herself, he was the sweetest guy she had ever met.

I was touched by her situation and gave her two pieces of advice- 1. Stop blaming yourself, he probably wasn't so good, if he was, he wouldn't have treated you that way over your past.

2. The book of proverbs says "discretion will preserve you". In your next relationship, be discreet. Discreet NOT Deceptive; Reveal everything at the appointed time.

More lessons from Esther

Loyalty: Esther was loyal to Mordecai her uncle; she was concerned when she heard about his sad countenance. Only a loyal and caring person would feel that way. Let us read: *"When Esther's maids and eunuchs came and told her about Mordecai, she was in great distress. She sent clothes for him to put on instead of his sackcloth, but he would not accept them. Then Esther summoned Hathach, one of the king's eunuchs assigned to attend her, and ordered him to find out what was troubling Mordecai and why." So Hathach went out to Mordecai in the open square of the city in front of the king's gate. Mordecai told him everything that had happened to him, including the exact amount of money Haman had promised to pay into the royal treasury for the destruction of the Jews. He also gave him a copy of the text of the edict for their annihilation, which had been published in Susa, to show to Esther and explain it to her, and he told him to urge her to go into the king's presence to beg for mercy and plead with him for her people. Hathach went back and* *reported to Esther what Mordecai had said. Then she instructed him to say to Mordecai, "All the king's officials and the people of the royal provinces know that for any man or woman who approaches the king in the inner court without being summoned the king has but one law: that he be put to death. The only exception to this is for the king to extend the gold scepter to him and spare his life. But thirty days have passed since I was called to go to the king." Est 4:4-11*

As we read on, we see that even though Esther didn't want to talk to the king because it was dangerous and could attract the death penalty, she still did so at the prompting of Mordecai. Some people despise the words of their counsellors or helpers once they get promoted, but not Esther; Esther hearkened to the voice of wisdom.

When Mordecai was told what Esther had said, he sent back this reply, "Don't think that you will escape being killed with the rest of the Jews, just because you live in the king's palace. If you don't speak up now, we will somehow get help, but you and your family will be killed. It could be that you were made queen for a time like this!" Est 4:12-14CEV.

Faith in God: Before Esther went to see the king, she requested that Mordecai and all Jews join her in fasting in prayer. That's really strategic; no wonder everything ended in praise, safety and promotion. Praying before taking any action is the way to go! Esther had faith in God. She knew that God's involvement would make all the difference.

"Then Esther sent this reply to Mordecai: "Go, gather together all the Jews who are in Susa, and fast for me. Do not eat

or drink for three days, night or day. I and my maids will fast as you do."

Courage: Courage is another lesson to learn from the life of Queen Esther. Courage is the ability to do what needs to be done even when you are afraid.

"All the king's officials and the people of the royal provinces know that for any man or woman who approaches the king in the inner court without being summoned the king has but one law: that he be put to death. The only exception to this is for the king to extend the gold sceptre to him and spare his life. But thirty days have passed since I was called to go to the king."

Esther knew how dangerous going to see the king uninvited could be, but she went anyway because the cause was right and her influence could make a difference.

"When this is done, I will go to the king, even though it is against the law. And if I perish, I perish." These were her words after instructing everyone to fast and pray.

Sensitivity and Wise: Esther was sensitive and strategic in making her petition known to the king. She realised that timing is very important.

"What do you wish, Queen Esther? What is your request? It shall be given to you — up to half the kingdom!"

*"If it pleases the king," replied Esther, "let the king, together with Haman, come today to a banquet I have prepared for him."*Est 5:3-4NIV

"What is your petition? It shall be granted you. What is your request, up to half the kingdom? It shall be done!" Esther replied, "My petition and my request is this: If the king regards me with favour and if it pleases the king to grant my petition and fulfil my request, let the king and Haman come tomorrow to the banquet I will prepare for them. Then I will answer the king's question." Est 5:6-8

*"What is your petition, Queen Esther? It shall be granted you. And what is your request, up to half the kingdom? It shall be done!"*Est 7:2

The first two times the king asked her what she wanted, she requested for his presence at her banquet; she knew how to gain more favour. By the third day, the king was probably more curious and determined to favour her.

Gracefulness*:* Esther always looked good. Make no mistakes about this; your appearance is as important as what you have to say. Always look your best, be dressed with grace and a happy, confident countenance. It will surprise you how easily you could get access to the palaces of life.

Dear single lady, there are certain kinds of men you cannot attract with stinking hair, bad breath or dirty clothes. So, take care of yourself; skincare and all, exfoliate, cleanse and apply makeup if you like. If you have poor dress sense, work on it.

Note: You are not under compulsion to improve on yourself, but I thought to mention it because, for some ladies, working on your appearance may just be the breakthrough you have been praying for.

It's not rocket science. If you want to be more attractive, make yourself more attractive. You don't have to break the bank or go into debt.

Hello wives, you are not exempt from the needful upgrade. I've seen women who stopped paying attention to their looks once they got married, but I think that is unnecessary. We have to keep looking attractive and hot.

You should also encourage your husband to look good, too. Everything seems new and interesting when they are taken care of. Pay attention and you will notice the magic a new singlet, short, bra, sleeping wear etc can create. Who else has noticed how hubby treats you more sweetly when you wear a new perfume or change your hairstyle or dress hot; now am blushing, I have been noticing my husband's smouldering stares and lingering pats since I returned from the salon. I think it's time for bed. I will write later.

Note that caring about your hygiene and how appealing you look to your husband is a sign of honour.

Naomi

Once upon a time — it was back in the days when judges led Israel — there was a famine in the land. A man from Bethlehem in Judah left home to live in the country of Moab, he and his wife and his two sons. The man's name was Elimelech; his wife's name was Naomi; his sons were named Mahlon and Kilion — all Ephrathites from Bethlehem in Judah. They all went to the country of Moab and settled there. Elimelech died and Naomi was left. She and her two sons. The sons took Moabite wives; the name of the first was Orpah, the second Ruth. They lived there in Moab for the next ten years. But then the two brothers, Mahlon and Kilion, died. Now the woman was left without either her young men or her husband. Ruth 1:1-5 MESSAGE*

With her two daughters-in-law, she left the place where she had been living and set out on the road that would take them back to the land of Judah. Then Naomi said to her two daughters-in-law, "Go back, each of you, to your mother's home. May the Lord show kindness to you, as you have shown to your dead and to me. May the Lord grant that each of you will find rest in the home of another husband." Then she kissed them and they wept aloud and said to her, "We will go back with you to your people.
Ruth 1:8-10 NIV*

From the relationship between Naomi and Ruth, we see that animosity between mothers-in-law and daughters-in-law is just a fable; it doesn't have to be anyone's reality.

Naomi was able to build a lasting relationship with her daughter-in-law that transcended their different tribes. Ruth was a Moabitess. This relationship led to Ruth fully adopting her as a mother, not a mother-in-law. It led to Ruth accepting her God as her own God.

The bond between Naomi and her daughter-in-law Ruth was so deep that the death of their connector; Naomi's son and Ruth's husband did not end it. It was so strong that moving to another country could not end it.

"But Ruth said: *Entreat me not to leave you, Or to turn back from following after you; For wherever you go, I will go; And wherever you lodge, I will lodge; Your people shall be my people, And your God, my God. Where you die, I will die, And there will I be buried. The Lord do so to me, and more also, If anything but death parts you and me."* Ruth 1:16-17(KJV)

Ruth's love and loyalty towards Naomi were born out of a great relationship and not from responsibility or legality. Loyalty is the rightful reward of love, not force. Legality cannot buy loyalty. Naomi was a kind and friendly woman who did not allow her loss to change her; she was committed to helping Ruth get a loving husband. Also, Naomi was Ruth's friend. She gave her counsel; they strategized and shared everything they had together.

It is a blessing to be a mother-in-law, but it is a greater blessing to be a mother to your daughter-in-law; it gives you the privilege to share a deeper connection that can only proceed out of genuine acceptance.

Every wise woman should want a sincere, deep and supportive relationship, whether as a mother-in-law or as a daughter-in-law.

> *The town women said to Naomi, "Blessed be God! He didn't leave you without family to carry on your life. May this baby grow up to be famous in Israel! He'll make you young again! He'll take care of you in old age. And this daughter-in-law who has brought him into the world and loves you so much, why, she's worth more to you than seven sons!"* Ruth 4:14-15THE MESSAGE.

Such a beautiful relationship can be freely enjoyed when we pay attention to these things:

- Our capacity to love
- Our ability to respond to love
- Our decision to freely give the gift of acceptance
- Our understanding of roles and obligations

1.Capacity to Love

We all have a different capacity to love, knowing this will help you work on yourself and increase your capacity to love if there's a need.

Some women can only love their biological children. It surprised a certain teacher who always felt abnormally angry and irritated by her pupils when, after self-examination, she found out that she could only have love and patience for her biological children.

Another woman, Anne, was having a turbulent relationship with her kids; during therapy, she realized she had never loved them. Surprising but true, despite birthing them, after so many years their relationship didn't get better. She always saw them as an outside force that came to steal her dreams, reduce her peace, snatch her joy and stress her.

I am happy to tell you that things changed for the better when she started working on enlarging her heart, i.e. increasing her capacity to accommodate others. Several stories abound to buttress this point, but suffice to say this could be the reason some mothers-in-law never accept or love their daughters-in-law and vice versa. This is the reason some people only care about themselves or their own or a few people.

Great relationships do not come with wishful thinking! To avoid any future frustration and misunderstanding, I must tell you the truth; It takes two to make a relationship work. If a kind, understanding mother-in-law meets a hateful, selfish daughter-in-law, it will be hard to create a beautiful relationship and vice versa. So, prayer and patience are vital. In terrible circumstances where the other party has refused to show civility and acceptance, I suggest you keep your distance while praying about it. That is better than trying to force it. Another thing that can help make things better is our willingness to embrace change.

Our different capacity to love is why everyone could never be Mother Teresa; this is the reason some people never make good spouses. Such a simple matter can be corrected easily, if only everyone knew.

2. Ability to respond to Love

The ability to respond to love is a skill you need to build a lasting relationship because if you don't know how to respond to love, it doesn't matter how nice others are to you, you will always be mean towards them and you will ruin beautiful relationships.

The danger of this is that even though love does not come with a condition of reciprocity, animosity can ruin it. Think about that and never get caught up with self-importance when others are sweet to you. Rather, enjoy love and give it back humbly.

3. Your decision to freely give the gift of acceptance

Freely giving the gift of acceptance is a testament to our ability to love. Dear mother-in-law, when you meet your daughter-in-law, try to see her as your daughter. Since your son has married her, it's better to accept her despite your inhibitions about her country, family background, educational qualification or looks. Dear daughter-in-law, you will do well to accept, love and honour the woman that birthed your husband. She deserves it; it is her due. Kindly recognise that on a scale from where you stand as a new wife, the weights are tipped in her favour.

This table is to show the uniqueness and importance of our roles and squelch the need for comparison.

Mother	Wife
She gave birth, raised and groomed him.	
She took care of him	

She educated him	
Friendship	Friendship
	Sex and intimacy: A mother has no business seeing her son naked and fully aroused. That area is under the jurisdiction of the wife.
Her time, finances and love were heavily invested before you came along.	Always remember, the mother has been playing key roles before you came upon the scene. You have a unique role, bask in it without competing and trying to usurp his mother.
Time has proven a mother's love and support.	Let time prove the wife's love and support. As time goes on her influence will increase.
	The wife will give birth to his children; something his mother won't do.

4. Understanding of roles and obligations

Understanding roles and obligations is an important aspect of building strong family ties.

Women are sensitive creations; we always love to do more than is required. I can't stop laughing as I write this, but seriously, whoever else has noticed this, kindly share your experience with me on my page.

Now, this characteristic of ours to do more than is required or usurp other people's roles sometimes causes issues when it is not properly harnessed.

As women, understanding our different roles at different times in the lives of others helps to execute them perfectly.

Mother – The premier caregiver, friend and supporter. No one has the power to choose their mother. It is a choice made by the sovereign God to entrust whom He will with.

Sister – Friend, supporter, advocate.

Colleague – If there's no defined love interest; it is always better to let things be professional.

Friend –Friendship between the opposite sex is always sensitive. It works better for all concerned when they set boundaries and define their relationship in clear terms.

Staff – Many people enjoy great working relationships without entanglements. It is safer not to mix business and pleasure.

Wife – My husband jokingly refers to me as his chief of staff because of how I can easily manage his affairs. The wife has the most all-encompassing role in the life of her husband. She is the only one that has the right to be sexually intimate with him. Every relationship between a man and other women does not have to be sexual except this. When a man marries a woman, it means he has automatically chosen her among others to be his partner.

This choice qualifies her to know more about him than anyone else. A man's decision will always affect his wife more than anyone else; a man should pray, plan and talk with his wife more than anyone else because she is the major stakeholder in his life.

Ruth

Ruth was a woman who rose above tragedy. Ruth was the daughter-in-law of Naomi and the widow of Chilhon. Ruth became the wife of Boaz and the mother of Obed; king David's granddad.

> *"Then Naomi said to her two daughters-in-law, "Go back, each of you, to your mother's home. May the Lord show kindness to you, as you have shown to your dead and to me. May the Lord grant that each of you will find rest in the home of another husband."* Ruth 1:8-9 NIV.

I don't think returning to her family makes Orpah a bad person or a rebel like some people like to insinuate. Even though what Ruth did was commendable, Orpah, didn't break any law or hurt anyone by going back. We don't know all the dynamics; perhaps Ruth didn't have the same relationships Orpah did. Besides, everyone processes grief differently. Some people may not want to dwell on their losses while some people like to reminisce and stay around those they share a common loss with.

> *At this, they wept again. Then Orpah kissed her mother-in-law goodbye, but Ruth clung to her. "Look," said Naomi, "your sister-in-law is going back to her people and her gods. Go back with her." But Ruth replied, "Don't urge me to leave you or to turn back from you. Where you go I will go, and where you stay I will stay. Your people will be my people and your God my God.*

Where you die I will die, and there I will be buried. May the Lord deal with me, be it ever so severely, if anything but death separates you and me." When Naomi realized Ruth was determined to go with her, she stopped urging her. Ruth 1:14-18NIV.

Now Naomi had a relative on her husband's side, from the clan of Elimelech, a man of standing, named Boaz.

The Working woman; Ruth didn't sit home all day. No, she did what her hands could find.

And Ruth the Moabitess said to Naomi, "Let me go to the fields and pick up the leftover grain behind anyone in whose eyes I find favour."

A kind and supportive mother-in-law

Naomi said to her, "Go ahead, my daughter." So she went out and began to glean in the fields behind the harvesters.

May you be led to good people.

As it turned out, she found herself working in a field belonging to Boaz, who was from the clan of Elimelech

The man Boaz: He was courteous. The bible recorded that he greeted the harvesters. He didn't come with an "I own the whole field" attitude. Secondly, Boaz was sensitive, he noticed a new face and made enquiries. Thirdly, Boaz knew how to encourage good behaviour, he was kinder to Ruth because he knew she deserved it for sticking with her mother-in-law.

Just then Boaz arrived from Bethlehem and greeted the harvesters, "The Lord be with you!" "The Lord bless you!" they called back. Boaz asked the foreman of his harvesters, "Whose young woman is that?" The foreman replied, "She is the Moabitess who came back from Moab with Naomi. She said, 'Please let me glean and gather among the sheaves behind the harvesters.' She went into the field and has worked steadily from morning till now, except for a short rest in the shelter."

<u>Choose a kind man: Boaz was kind to Ruth without any strings attached.</u> There were no sexual innuendos or the likes because he was a good man. Hello, kindness and God-fearing are the major labels to look out for.

So Boaz said to Ruth, "My daughter, listen to me. Don't go and glean in another field and don't go away from here. Stay here with my servant girls. Watch the field where the men are harvesting, and follow along after the girls. I have told the men not to touch you. And whenever you are thirsty, go and get a drink from the water jars the men have filled." At this, she bowed down with her face to the ground. She exclaimed, "Why have I found such favour in your eyes that you notice me — a foreigner?" Boaz replied, "I've been told all about what you have done for your mother-in-law since the death of your husband — how you left your father and mother and your homeland and came to live with a people you did not know before. May the Lord repay you for what you have done. May you be richly rewarded by the Lord, the God of Israel, under whose wings you have come to take refuge."

"May I continue to find favour in your eyes, my lord," she said. "You have given me comfort and have spoken kindly to your servant — though I do not have the standing of one of your servant girls." At mealtime, Boaz said to her, "Come over here. Have some bread and dip it in the wine vinegar."

When she sat down with the harvesters, he offered her some roasted grain. She ate all she wanted and had some leftover. As she got up to glean, Boaz gave orders to his men, "Even if she gathers among the sheaves, don't embarrass her. Rather, pull out some stalks for her from the bundles and leave them for her to pick up, and don't rebuke her." So Ruth gleaned in the field until evening. Then she threshed the barley she had gathered, and it amounted to about an ephah. She carried it back to town, and her mother-in-law saw how much she had gathered. Ruth also brought out and gave her what she had left over after she had eaten enough. Her mother-in-law asked her, "Where did you glean today? Where did you work? Blessed be the man who took notice of you!"

<u>A friend in a mother-in-law; Ruth was free to talk about how her day went.</u>

Then Ruth told her mother-in-law about the one at whose place she had been working. "The name of the man I worked with today is Boaz," she said. "The Lord bless him!" Naomi said to her daughter-in-law. "He has not stopped showing his kindness to the living and the dead." She added, "That man is our close relative; he is one of our kinsman-redeemers." Then Ruth the Moabitess said, "He even said to me, 'Stay with my workers until they finish harvesting all my grain." Naomi said to Ruth her daughter-in-law, "It will be good for you, my daughter, to go with his girls, because in someone else's field you might be harmed." So Ruth stayed close to the servant girls of Boaz to glean until the barley and wheat harvests were finished. And she lived with her mother-in-law. Ruth 2:1-23NIV

The Strategy; the love of a mother

One day, her mother-in-law Naomi said to Ruth, "My dear daughter, isn't it about time I arranged a good home for you so you can have a happy life? And isn't Boaz our close relative, the one with whose young women you've been working? Maybe it's time to make our move. Tonight is the night of Boaz's barley harvest at the threshing floor.

"Take a bath. Put on some perfume. Get all dressed up and go to the threshing floor. But don't let him know you're there until the party is well underway, and he's had plenty of food and drink. When you see him slipping off to sleep, watch where he lies down and then go there. Lie at his feet to let him know that you are available to him for marriage. Then wait and see what he says. He'll tell you what to do." Ruth said, "If you say so, I'll do it, just as you've told me." She went down to the threshing floor <u>and put her mother-in-law's plan into action</u>. Boaz had a good time eating and drinking his fill — he felt great. Then he went off to get some sleep, lying down at the end of a stack of barley. Ruth quietly followed; she lay down to signal her availability for marriage. In the middle of the night, the man was suddenly startled and sat up. Surprise! This woman asleep at his feet! Ruth 3:1-8THE MESSAGE.

Naomi, Ruth's mother-in-law, counselled her rightly and Ruth, on her part, listened and acted on the counsel.

Did you notice that Ruth did not wait for Boaz to court her, rather she made herself available for a good relationship? And because she chose Boaz, who was a good man, it ended in honour and blessing. Before you try to put yourself on display for a man who has not shown interest, ensure you do your homework and get the right counsel; choose a good man – or it may end in tears. The average man is a hunter and may prefer to go for what he wants, but certain men are too busy or distracted to go for what they want and it's never a bad idea to help them see you... do it with discretion.

> *"So Boaz took Ruth, and she was his wife: and when he went in unto her, the Lord gave her conception, and she bare a son. And the women said unto Naomi, Blessed be the Lord, which hath not left thee this day without a kinsman, that his name may be famous in Israel. And he shall be unto thee a restorer of thy life, and a nourisher of thine old age: for thy daughter in law, which loveth thee, which is better to thee than seven sons, hath born him. And Naomi took the child, and laid it in her bosom, and became nurse unto it. And the women her neighbours gave it a name, saying, There is a son born to Naomi; and they called his name Obed: he is the father of Jesse, the father of David."*

I celebrate the love Ruth had for her mother-in-law, Naomi. It was plain for all to see. I bless the Lord for His kindness. Despite everything Ruth and Naomi went through, it ended in praise.

After this, Paul left Athens and went to Corinth. There he met a Jew named Aquila, a native of Pontus, who had recently come from Italy with his wife Priscilla because Claudius had ordered all the Jews to leave Rome. Paul went to see them, and because he was a tentmaker as they were, he stayed and worked with them. Every Sabbath he reasoned in the synagogue, trying to persuade Jews and Greeks. Acts 18:1-4 NIV

Every time we saw the name of Priscilla, we also saw the name of Aquila, her husband. I thought it worthy of note because some couples cannot serve together in the same parish; some cannot work together in the same committee. Some cannot work together in the same church without fighting each other or using their unity to fight against others. But not Priscilla and Aquila. They were both sold out to the preaching of the gospel. Every time their names came up, it concerned outstanding service, selflessness and impact.

Paul stayed on in Corinth for some time. Then he left the brothers and sailed for Syria, accompanied by Priscilla and Aquila. Before he sailed, he had his hair cut off at Cenchrea because of a vow he had taken. They arrived at Ephesus, where Paul left Priscilla and Aquila. Acts 18:18-19 NIV

When Priscilla and Aquila heard him, they invited him to their home and explained to him the way of God more adequately. Acts 18:26 NIV.

The churches in the province of Asia send you greetings. Aquila and Priscilla greet you warmly in the Lord, and so does the church that meets at their house. 1 Cor 16:19-20 NIV.

Greet Priscilla and Aquila and the household of Onesiphorus. 2 Tim 4:19 NIV,

Greet Priscilla and Aquila, my fellow workers in Christ Jesus. They risked their lives for me. Not only I but all the churches of the Gentiles are grateful to them. Greet also the church that meets at their house. Rom 16:3-4 NIV.

Priscilla and her husband used everything they had to serve the Lord. As a couple, they were in sync, sold out to God and being a blessing. They even had a church in their house! Shout out to couples serving God together; keeping it real, enjoying a beautiful marriage and putting Jesus at the centre of their lives.

Priscilla and Aquila were so amazing that Apostle Paul just loved sending them greetings. When you read how frequently he wrote about them, you could tell that he was so blessed by their ministry, he could not stop bragging about their selflessness and good deeds.

Peter's Mother-in-law

When Jesus came into Peter's home, He saw his mother-in-law lying sick in bed with a fever. He touched her hand, and the fever left her; and she got up and waited on Him. Matt 8:14-16 NASU

Saved to serve. This is the reason behind your miracles, blessings, strength, restoration, ability and prosperity. YOU ARE SAVED TO SERVE. So, start serving. Nothing is too small and nothing is too grand. Just use what you have to do the Master's bidding.

Peter's mother-in-law was not a young woman, yet she served. She did not use her age as an excuse.

Peter's mother-in-law didn't serve because there was no else to serve. So, even if a million people are already doing what you would want to do, still do yours. Serving is personal, we all might do the same thing, but there's always a uniqueness about every work.

Serving is the highest form of gratitude. Has God been good to you? Serve him.

Your serving is tied to your relevance, and your relevance is tied to your promotion. The more you serve, the better you become.

The message translation says, *"He touched her hand and the fever was gone. No sooner was she up on her feet than she was fixing dinner for him.* Matt 8:15 MSB

She made dinner for the Lord. What is your own area of competence? What can you do? Everyone must not stand behind the pulpit, write a book or hold city-wide crusades. But everyone has a role to play. From those who provide support, check on others, take care of the logistics and planning, give financially, show love and kindness, visit the sick and elderly, share their food with others, visit the prisons, etc. We do not know enough to say which roles are the most important, but we know it is more beautiful when everyone does what they can. Have you ever felt hungry after a meeting where you were preaching the Word and healing the sick? If you have, then, the fact that Peter's mother-in-law "prepared dinner" and it was written in the bible will make more sense to you.

Be a blessing in your own unique way.

Phoebe

I commend to you our sister Phoebe, a servant of the church in Cenchrea. I ask you to receive her in the Lord in a way worthy of the saints and to give her any help she may need from you, for she has been a great help to many people, including me. Rom 16:1-2

Phoebe reminds me of the saying, "One good turn deserves another". Did you notice that Apostle Paul asked them to give her all the help she may need because she is a helpful, wonderful and kind person? If you were to be paid in your coin today, would it be a good one? Would you love to receive a harvest of the seeds you are sowing? Are you sowing seeds of kindness and love?

Some people get so nervous at the thought of anyone analysing their deeds. They throw the "do not judge" sentence around like a shield. And practically start quarrelling whenever anyone suggests people should be treated how they treat others. I am never in support of retaliation, but I am particularly concerned about the dangers of raising an irresponsible generation. The average person will try anything if they think they will get away with it. We shouldn't indirectly encourage people to hurt others. When we fight aggrieved persons more than offenders, that is what we are doing. True love, liberality and maturity are not displayed when we defend wrongdoers and shun equity or morality. So, let's create a balance instead.

Zelophehad's Daughters

Zelophehad son of Hepher had no sons; he had only daughters, whose names were Mahlah, Noah, Hoglah, Milcah and Tirzah.) Num 26:33 NIV

Then came the daughters of Zelophehad the son of Hepher, the son of Gilead, the son of Machir, the son of Manasseh, from the families of Manasseh the son of Joseph; and these were the names of his daughters: Mahlah, Noah, Hoglah, Milcah, and Tirzah. And they stood before Moses, before Eleazar the priest, and before the leaders and all the congregation, by the doorway of the tabernacle of meeting, saying: "Our father died in the wilderness; but he was not in the company of those who gathered together against the Lord, in company with Korah, but he died in his own sin, and he had no sons. Why should the name of our father be removed from among his family because he had no son? Give us a possession among our father's brothers."

So Moses brought their case before the Lord. And the Lord spoke to Moses, saying: "The daughters of Zelophehad speak what is right; you shall surely give them a possession of inheritance among their father's brothers and cause the inheritance of their father to pass to them. And you shall speak to the children of Israel, saying: 'If a man dies and has no son, then you shall cause his inheritance to pass to his daughter. Num 27:1-9NKJV.

A lot of societies in different parts of the world do not allow women to inherit their father's belongings. The worst part of it is that some of these societies claim to be following the Bible. I wonder how they could have missed this divine judicial precedent or perhaps they are fully aware and are just letting greed govern them?

Gender inequality is backed by greed and inferiority complex, not God. Deliberate wrong interpretation of scriptures and blatant denial of the true counsel of God by some leaders has left several people with the impression that God does not care about women and that the bible supports laws that hurt women.

> *There was not a woman in that country as beautiful as Job's daughters. Their father treated them as equals with their brothers, providing the same inheritance.* Job 42:15 Message

#

"Now Sarai Abram's wife bare him no children: and she had an handmaid, an Egyptian, whose name was Hagar. And Sarai said unto Abram, Behold now, the Lord hath restrained me from bearing: I pray thee, go in unto my maid; it may be that I may obtain children by her. And Abram hearkened to the voice of Sarai. And Sarai Abram's wife took Hagar her maid the Egyptian, after Abram had dwelt ten years in the land of Canaan, and gave her to her husband Abram to be his wife." Gen 16:1-3

Hagar is symbolic of women without rights, women who don't have a say concerning what happens in their lives. This lack of rights could be because of the circumstances of their lives, their place of birth, cultural, religious, financial or educational, and social factors.

When Sarah gave Hagar her maid to Abraham, Hagar's opinion was not sought, because it was not relevant. After all, she was a slave. Slavery is living life based on the terms of others, being at the mercy of their whims, caprices, and decisions. Any relationship where you are laden with responsibility and denied the right to have expectations is slavery, albeit in disguise.

A healthy relationship is one where boundaries are defined, where you are protected, where you have some level of control over decisions concerning your life, where the option of being maltreated and cast out is not the first option whenever you make a mistake. Rather, love and correction are the first recourse.

And he went in <u>unto Hagar, and she conceived: and when she saw</u> <u>that she had conceived, her mistress was despised in her eyes.</u> And Sarai said unto Abram, My wrong be upon thee: I have given my maid into thy bosom; and when she saw that she had conceived, I was despised in her eyes: the Lord judge between me and thee. But Abram said unto Sarai, Behold, thy maid is in thy hand; do to her as it pleaseth thee. And when Sarai dealt hardly with her, she fled from her face. <u>And the angel of the Lord found her by a fountain of water in the</u> <u>wilderness, by the fountain in the way to Shur. And he said, Hagar,</u> <u>Sarai's maid, whence camest thou? And whither wilt thou go? And</u> <u>she said, I flee from the face of my mistress Sarai. And the angel of</u> <u>the Lord said unto her, Return to thy mistress, and submit thyself</u> <u>under her hands. And the angel of the Lord said unto her, I will</u> <u>multiply thy seed exceedingly, that it shall not be numbered for</u> <u>multitude.11 And the angel of the Lord said unto her, Behold, thou art</u> <u>with child, and shalt bear a son, and shalt call his name Ishmael;</u> <u>because the Lord hath heard thy affliction.</u> Gen 16:4-11.

Verse 4 shows the Error of Hagar. She forgot where she was coming from. She forgot her position. She forgot Sarah was her boss and got carried away by her momentary success. She forgot there was a time and way to negotiate. She forgot: **Rule Number 2, Never Fight The One Who Made Room For You.**

Hagar might have made a mistake by disrespecting her mistress, but God is compassionate and just. The angel of the Lord visited, counselled and strengthened Hagar; God cares about everyone, even Hagar who was called a slave. He assured her of His love. God is always looking out for us.

Hagar found a friend in God; He asked her what was going on, even though He already knew. He instructed her to go back and mend her ways by submitting herself to her mistress. He comforts her with a promise of increase and prosperity. He told her about her future and named her son Ishmael because He had heard her affliction. And Hagar did as the Lord instructed her.

She gave this name to the Lord who spoke to her: "You are the God who sees me," for she said, "I have now seen the One who sees me." That is why the well was called Beer Lahai Roi; it is still there, between Kadesh and Bered. So Hagar bore Abram a son, and Abram gave the name Ishmael to the son she had borne. Abram was eighty-six years old when Hagar bore him Ishmael. Gen 16:13-16 NIV.

Have you found a friend in Jesus? Will you let Him befriend, provide for and protect you? Will you receive His counsel and His Word. He is merciful and kind. Loving and righteous. He gives beauty for ashes. Strength for fear. Joy for mourning. Peace for depression. You are special to God; He loves you so much and does not care about your past or background the way the enemy wants you to think He does.

Manoah's Wife

Manoah's wife was Samson's mother. She was a woman of good understanding and great faith.

> *Now there was a certain man from Zorah, of the family of the Danites, whose name was Manoah; and his wife was barren and had no children. And the Angel of the Lord appeared to the woman and said to her, "Indeed now, you are barren and have borne no children, but you shall conceive and bear a son. Now therefore, please be careful not to drink wine or similar drink, and not to eat anything unclean. For behold, you shall conceive and bear a son. And no razor shall come upon his head, for the child shall be a Nazirite to God from the womb; and he shall begin to deliver Israel out of the hand of the Philistines".*

Isn't it amazing that the angel met the woman right where she was? Sometimes women fret about not having enough quiet time to meet with God; some even see their husbands and children as hindrances to their spiritual advancement. I think that is an error-raising Godly children is as important an assignment as any other. Develop a healthy schedule that involves your family and you will still find time for deep meditations, especially as your children grow and understand the importance of God.

Manoah's wife didn't have to go anywhere or pray up a storm. All she seemed to do was go about her normal day with a clean, beautiful heart. Sometimes God comes to us because we prayed and pleaded for visitation, but sometimes He comes to us because of His purpose for us. God has a purpose for every life and it is important we realise He will bring His purpose to pass. All we have to do is respond to His lead and follow His instructions. One thing that amazes me about the bible and every individual's account is the fact that no two stories are alike.

> *So the woman came and told her husband, saying,'' A Man of God came to me, and His countenance was like the countenance of the Angel of God, very awesome; but I did not ask Him where He was from, and He did not tell me His name. And He said to me, 'Behold, you shall conceive and bear a son. Now drink no wine or similar drink, nor eat anything unclean, for the child shall be a Nazirite to God from the womb to the day of his death.''* Judges 13:2-7

Manoah's wife believed the Word that was said to her and shared the good news with her husband. How sweet. Her husband prayed God would send the angel again, and he came again to the woman.

> *Then Manoah prayed to the Lord, and said, "O my Lord, please let the Man of God whom You sent come to us again and teach us what we shall do for the child who will be born." And God listened to the voice of Manoah, and the Angel of God came to the woman again as she was sitting in the field; but Manoah her husband was not with her. Then the woman ran in haste and told her husband, and said to him, "Look, the Man who came to me the other day has just now appeared to me!" So Manoah*

arose and followed his wife. When he came to the Man, he said to Him, "Are You the Man who spoke to this woman?"

And He said, "I am." Manoah said, "Now let Your words come to pass! What will be the boy's rule of life, and his work?"

So the Angel of the Lord said to Manoah, "Of all that I said to the woman, let her be careful. She may not eat anything that comes from the vine, nor may she drink wine or similar drink, nor eat anything unclean. All that I commanded her let her observe."

Then Manoah said to the Angel of the Lord, "Please let us detain You, and we will prepare a young goat for You." And the Angel of the Lord said to Manoah, "Though you detain Me, I will not eat your food. But if you offer a burnt offering, you must offer it to the Lord." (For Manoah did not know He was the Angel of the Lord.) Judg 13:8-16

Then Manoah asked the angel of the Lord, "What is your name? For when all this comes true, we want to honour you."

"Why do you ask my name?" the angel of the Lord replied. <u>"It is too wonderful for you to understand."</u>

Then Manoah took a young goat and a grain offering and offered it on a rock as a sacrifice to the Lord. And as Manoah and his wife watched, the Lord did an amazing thing. As the flames from the altar shot up toward the sky, the angel of the Lord ascended in the fire. When Manoah and his wife saw this, they fell with their faces to the ground. The angel did not appear again to Manoah and his wife. Manoah finally realized it was the *angel of the Lord, and he said to his wife, "We will certainly die, for we have seen God!"*Judg 13:16-22

The next verse is why I say she is a woman of good understanding and great faith.

But his wife said, "If the Lord were going to kill us, he wouldn't have accepted our burnt offering and grain offering. He wouldn't have appeared to us and told us this wonderful thing and done these miracles." When her son was born, she named him Samson. And the Lord blessed him as he grew up. And the Spirit of the Lord began to stir him while he lived in Mahaneh-dan, which is located between the towns of Zorah and Eshtaol. Judge 13:23-25

The angel of the Lord's description of Himself when Manoah asked Him His name does something beautiful to me every time I read it, He said, "It is too wonderful for you to understand". The Message translation says, "It is sheer wonder", God is indeed beyond description.

Queen of the South - Queen of Sheba

"And when the queen of Sheba heard of the fame of Solomon concerning the name of the Lord, she came to prove him with hard questions. And she came to Jerusalem with a very great train, with camels that bare spices, and very much gold, and precious stones: and when she was come to Solomon, she communed with him of all that was in her heart. And Solomon told her all her questions: there was not any thing hid from the king, which he told her not. And when the queen of Sheba had seen all Solomon's wisdom, and the house that he had built, And the meat of his table, and the sitting of his servants, and the attendance of his ministers, and their apparel, and his cupbearers, and his ascent by which he went up unto the house of the Lord; there was no more spirit in her. And she said to the king, It was a true report that I heard in mine own land of thy acts and of thy wisdom. Howbeit I believed not the words, until I came, and mine eyes had seen it: and, behold, the half was not told me; thy wisdom and prosperity exceedeth the fame which I heard. Happy are thy men, happy are these thy servants, which stand continually before thee, and that hear thy wisdom. Blessed be the Lord thy God, which delighted in thee, to set thee on the throne of Israel: because the Lord loved Israel forever, therefore made He thee king, to do judgment and justice. And she gave the king an hundred and twenty talents of gold, and of spices

very great store, and precious stones: there came no more such abundance of spices as these which the queen of Sheba gave to king Solomon. And the navy also of Hiram, that brought gold from Ophir, brought in from Ophir great plenty of almug trees, and precious stones. And the king made of the almug trees pillars for the house of the Lord, and for the king's house, harps also and psalteries for singers: there came no such almug trees, nor were seen unto this day. And king Solomon gave unto the queen of Sheba all her desire, whatsoever she asked, beside that which Solomon gave her of his royal bounty. So she turned and went to her own country, she and her servants." 1 Kings 10:1-13

The queen of Sheba, also referred to as the queen of the south in the New Testament, shows that being female is not grounds for being ignorant. She understands that being royalty should not stop you from recognising that there are greater levels of glory.

Distance is not an excuse; no excuse is good enough. We must seek knowledge. We read that she came prepared; bearing gifts of honour, an open heart to learn, investigate and see if such graces of which she had heard existed. She came to prove him with hard questions.

When she saw the excellence by which things were done, she was flabbergasted. Look at the underlined verse... Isn't it symbolic that the queen of Sheba got all she wanted?

Our Lord Jesus said in Matt. 12:42 that *"The queen of the south shall rise up in the judgment with this generation, and shall condemn it: for she came from the uttermost parts of the earth to hear the wisdom of Solomon; and, behold, a greater than Solomon is here."*

Hallelujah! A greater than Solomon is here. Are you doing all you need to do to know Him? Do you have time for fellowship? Do you bask in the sheer wonder of His grace, love, and power? Do you seek Him tirelessly through the study of your bible? Do you give gifts of love befitting His majesty- knowing fully well that He will give you back even more than you could ever ask for? He will give you your heart's desires according to His good words.

Are you still arguing about the need to worship and serve in a sanctuary, because you don't enjoy leaving your house, or do you think you are too busy?

Are you still arguing about tithing and every form of giving? Do you think the world revolves around you only?

I hope not, sister. I hope not, brother. A greater than Solomon is here, He is Jesus Christ. Don't be among those the queen of the south shall rise in judgment of and condemn. For she came from the uttermost parts of the earth to hear the wisdom of Solomon. Thou are without an excuse.

Jephthah's Daughter

And Jephthah made a vow to the Lord: "If you give the Ammonites into my hands, whatever comes out of the door of my house to meet me when I return in triumph from the Ammonites will be the Lord's, and I will sacrifice it as a burnt offering." Then Jephthah went over to fight the Ammonites, and the Lord gave them into his hands. He devastated twenty towns from Aroer to the vicinity of Minnith, as far as Abel Keramim. Thus Israel subdued Ammon. When Jephthah returned to his home in Mizpah, who should come out to meet him but his daughter, dancing to the sound of tambourines! She was an only child. Except for her, he had neither son nor daughter. When he saw her, he tore his clothes and cried, "Oh! My daughter! You have made me miserable and wretched, because I have made a vow to the Lord that I cannot break."

"My father," she replied, "<u>you have given your word to the Lord. Do to me just as you promised,</u> now that the Lord has avenged you of your enemies, the Ammonites. But grant me this one request," she said. "Give me two months to roam the hills and weep with my friends, because I will never marry."

"You may go," he said. And he let her go for two months. She and the girls went into the hills and wept because she would never marry. After the two months, she returned to her father and he did to her as he had vowed. And she was a virgin.

From this comes the Israelite custom that each year the young women of Israel go out for four days to commemorate the daughter of Jephthah the Gileadite. Judg 11:30-40 NIV.

Jephthah's daughter's obedience became a memorial, and rightly so because she paid the ultimate price for honour. She chose to obey her father. Obedience to the call of duty is not always pleasant. Sometimes keeping your word seems like the hardest thing, then imagine if it was not your word in the first place; Jephthah's daughter wasn't the one who pledged to God, yet she agreed to be a sacrifice.

How far would you go to keep your family's honour? How far would you go to help someone else keep his word?

Jephthah's daughter sure went far. Some people believed she was offered by being killed, some others believe her being offered meant living a life of seclusion all her life; hence her request, *"But first let me do this one thing: Let me go up and roam in the hills and weep with my friends for two months, because I will die a virgin " "You may go," Jephthah said. And he sent her away for two months. She and her friends went into the hills and wept because she would never have children. When she returned home, her father kept the vow he had made, and she died a virgin".* Judg 11:37-39.

Peninnah

Now there was a certain man of Ramathaim Zophim, of the mountains of Ephraim, and his name was Elkanah the son of Jeroham, the son of Elihu, the son of Tohu, the son of Zuph, an Ephraimite. And he had two wives: the name of one was Hannah, and the name of the other Peninnah. Peninnah had children, but Hannah had no children. 1 Sam 1:1-2 NKJV

When Elkanah sacrificed, he passed helpings from the sacrificial meal around to his wife Peninnah and all her children, but he always gave an especially generous helping to Hannah because he loved her so much, and because God had not given her children. But her rival wife taunted her cruelly, rubbing it in and never letting her forget that God had not given her children. 1 Sam 1:4-7 MESSAGE

Peninnah was a mocker- a mocker is someone who teases others about a lack in their life just to hurt them. A mocker is someone who treats others with contempt or derision. Mockers always have a patronising attitude or condescending air about them. They are highly critical and unnecessarily sarcastic.

A mocker is someone who derives joy from ridiculing others. When someone sees you as a rival, they would always compare their life with yours. As they run their race, they always look over their shoulder to ensure others are far behind. The thought that someone else could be happier than them torments them and so they always love to remind others about something they do not have. They ask questions like:

Does she have a better job?
Does she enjoy the admiration and attention of a man?
How many degrees does she have?
Is she married?
Does she have children? What is their sex? Are my kids older?
What kind of car does she drive? How influential is she? Etc.

Some years back, I went to a store to get a pair of shoes for my baby girl. There I met a woman ridiculing my choice of shoes and insisting I take another one. It seemed she was asking me to take it because it was extravagantly priced. Incidentally, I didn't want that shoe because my baby already has that exact design, and was even wearing it that day. I didn't know this woman from anywhere; she was not the owner of the store or an attendant, yet she kept dropping caustic comments about people looking richer than they are. While I was pondering on her rude attitude and thinking about asking someone to bring my princess from the car just to shock her into minding her business, another woman walked in with her daughter, a beautiful 7year old.

Amazingly, they were casual acquaintances. The lady with the rude attitude immediately started berating the other woman about her daughter's weight and other things, "This girl is too fat. What is this now? This is not proper. From my calculations, she is not over seven... You don't love this child. If you do, you would realise that a girl should be slim and stop feeding her too much nonsense," she said. I was perplexed, but that was not all. She wasn't nearly done. She continued, "By the way, this girl is seven. When are you going to have another child; she should have at least 2 younger siblings now, but no, you are feeding her fat instead and having parties?" I felt sorry for the other woman as she tried to explain that the party her husband told her husband about was to celebrate her 7th birthday.

I felt so angry and wanted to talk to her, but I didn't know where to start, especially since I already acted like I wasn't Igbo. I did that because I didn't want to get familiar with her. I had met no one so brazenly mean before. Amid her vituperations, she would laugh and say, "adaa me kwu nke nzuzo, strong women say it as it is". Truth is, there is nothing strong about being insensitive and hurtful. She was a bitter woman who found solace in mocking others. Several women mock others in varying degrees; please pass the memo, "It has to stop, you should not highlight others supposed 'inadequacy'. If you do, then it's better not to arrogate a "strong woman" title to yourself."

Imagine if that lady was having difficulty conceiving and her fellow woman now came to add to her pain. She had no right to talk to anybody that way, especially her acquaintances. Emotional abuse is abuse.

Dorcas

Now there was at Joppa a certain disciple named Tabitha, which by interpretation is called Dorcas: this woman was full of good works and alms deeds which she did. And it came to pass in those days, that she was sick, and died: whom when they had washed, they laid her in an upper chamber. And forasmuch as Lydda was nigh to Joppa, and the disciples had heard that Peter was there, they sent unto him two men, desiring him that he would not delay to come to them. Then Peter arose and went with them. When he was come, they brought him into the upper chamber: and all the widows stood by him weeping, and shewing the coats and garments which Dorcas made, while she was with them. But Peter put them all forth, and kneeled down, and prayed; and turning him to the body said, Tabitha, arise. And she opened her eyes: and when she saw Peter, she sat up. And he gave her his hand, and lifted her up, and when he had called the saints and widows, presented her alive. And it was known throughout all Joppa; and many believed in the Lord. And it came to pass, that he tarried many days in Joppa with one Simon a tanner. "Acts 9:36-43.

Dorcas, also called Tabitha, had an inspiring introduction, *"This woman was full of good works and alms deeds which she did."*

Tabitha's good work spoke for her when she couldn't speak for herself. Her good works inspired her resurrection.

If every one of us is kind, the world will be a better place. I heard a story about a woman. I will call her Mrs. Lovelyn. She had a neighbour who was a missionary from another African country. On a certain day, as Mrs Lovelyn passed by the window of her neighbour's house, she heard her praying and crying to God to bless her with a certain amount of money; she was pouring out her heart with so much anguish because she believed she was alone and no one else could hear her.

Mrs Lovelyn was so shaken by her neighbour's heartfelt prayer because she felt it was not an enormous amount of money. She wanted to help, but she didn't know how. She couldn't possibly say, "I heard you praying about your family needs so I want to help". It may make her neighbour feel embarrassed. So, she prayed about it and God gave her a strategy. So, she took the exact amount of money and stealthily observed her neighbour. When she knew she wouldn't be seen, she threw the wrapped money inside the house and walked away. A few minutes later, she had a loud shout that reverberated through the building. When she ran out to ask what had happened, she saw it was her neighbour giving praise to God for His faithfulness. Her neighbour shared how she walked into her room and found the exact sum of money she had been praying to God about. She was amazed and gave glory to God.

To date, no one in that family knows how that miracle came about. But God, who sees in secret, knows all things. When you get interested in being a channel of blessing, nothing can stop you.

You will fulfil the scripture that says men will see your good works and glorify your Father in heaven.

Choose to be used by God, choose to be an answer to someone's prayer. Be a helper and not just someone praying for help. Let love, help, gifts, kindness, money and every good thing never be scarce rather let it go round because of you. Say no to needless suffering. And God will reward you beautifully.

Tamar (Judah's daughter-in-law)

Judah got a wife for Er, his firstborn. Her name was Tamar. But Judah's firstborn, Er, grievously offended God and God took his life. So Judah told Onan, "Go and sleep with your brother's widow; it's the duty of a brother-in-law to keep your brother's line alive." But Onan knew that the child wouldn't be his, so whenever he slept with his brother's widow he spilled his semen on the ground so he wouldn't produce a child for his brother. God was much offended by what he did and also took his life. So Judah stepped in and told his daughter-in-law Tamar, "Live as a widow at home with your father until my son Shelah grows up." He was worried that Shelah would also end up dead, just like his brothers. So Tamar went to live with her father.

Time passed. Judah's wife, Shua's daughter, died. When the time of mourning was over, Judah with his friend Hirah of Adullam went to Timnah for the sheep shearing.

She said, "What will you pay me?"

"I'll send you," he said, "a kid goat from the flock."

She said, "Not unless you give me a pledge until you send it."
"So what would you want in the way of a pledge?"

She said, "Your personal seal-and-cord and the staff you carry." He handed them over to her and slept with her. And she got pregnant. She then left and went home. She removed her veil and put her widow's clothes back on.

Judah sent the kid goat by his friend from Adullam to recover the pledge from the woman. But he couldn't find her. He asked the men of that place, "Where's the prostitute that used to sit by the road here near Enaim?"

They said, "There's never been a prostitute here." He went back to Judah and said, "I couldn't find her. The men there said there never has been a prostitute there."

Judah said, "Let her have it then. If we keep looking, everyone will be poking fun at us. I kept my part of the bargain — I sent the kid goat but you couldn't find her."

Three months or so later, Judah was told, "Your daughter-in-law has been playing the whore — and now she's a pregnant whore."

Judah yelled, "Get her out here. Burn her up!"

When she was brought out, she sent to her father-in-law, saying, "By the man to whom these belong, I am with child." And she said," Please determine whose these are — the signet and cord, and staff." So Judah acknowledged them and said, "She has been more righteous than I, because I did not give her to Shelah my son." And he never knew her again.

Now it came to pass, at the time for giving birth, that behold, twins were in her womb. And so it was, when she was giving birth, that the one put out his hand; and the midwife took a scarlet thread and bound it on his hand, saying, "This one came out first." Then it happened, as he drew back his hand, that his brother came out unexpectedly; and she said, "How did you break through? This breach be upon you!" Therefore his name was called Perez. Afterward his brother came out who had the scarlet thread on his hand. And his name was called Zerah. Gen 38:25-30

Tamar was a perfect example of what desperation can make one do. To be desperate means to lose hope. Desperation makes people do things they may never have thought possible. In Tamar's case, it made her strategize to sleep with her father-in-law.

Tamar became the mother of Perez and Zerah through sheer determination. What she did was so risky it could have caused her death. Her actions reminded me of a class I had during my law studies. In that class, we were told that there are factors that determine justice; two people can commit the same crime and yet suffer different consequences. They categorised these factors as mitigating and aggravating factors. Tamar's action could be termed incense and prostitution, but they were not. It seemed more fitting to call her the woman who was desperate enough to get her rights. Or the woman who refused to be cheated.

Virginity and Women's Rights

Sometimes it may look like sexual purity should be observed by women alone. But I think everyone that cares about their life should observe sexual purity. A young girl felt saddened because she thought her mom was practising gender inequality by policing her to go back home early every time she goes out. She asked a question, "Is it important for the boys to be virgins too? If men can have sex indiscriminately, why shouldn't I?"

First, read the chapter on strange women so you can understand that men are expected to live holy lives; they were also warned severally to desist from casual sex because of the dangers. The young lady's question arose because of the misconception that only females ought to be virtuous. It was not a straightforward question to answer, but I think God's rules were created more for our protection and not to inhibit us. If the need to be pure seems to be more expected and demanded of females, I believe there is a good reason. We don't know as much as God, our creator; so it is best to follow the operating manual our creator has made available.

We cannot overemphasise the difference between female and male reproductive organs. A man can impregnate several women over a 9month period. When a man impregnates a woman and you see him six months afterwards, there are no physical changes to show what he did, but the life and body of the woman changes drastically. I think the benefits of being a virgin is underrated.

"If any man takes a wife, and goes in to her, and detests her, and charges her with shameful conduct, and brings a bad name on her, and says, 'I took this woman, and when I came to her I found she was not a virgin,' then the father and mother of the young woman shall take and bring out the evidence of the young woman's virginity to the elders of the city at the gate. And the young woman's father shall say to the elders, 'I gave my daughter to this man as wife, and he detests her. Now he has charged her with shameful conduct, saying, "I found your daughter was not a virgin," and yet these are the evidences of my daughter's virginity.' And they shall spread the cloth before the elders of the city. Then the elders of that city shall take that man and punish him; and they shall fine him one hundred shekels of silver and give them to the father of the young woman, because he has brought a bad name on a virgin of Israel. And she shall be his wife; he cannot divorce her all his days. "But if the thing is true, and evidences of virginity are not found for the young woman, then they shall bring out the young woman to the door of her father's house, and the men of her city shall stone her to death with stones, because she has done a disgraceful thing in Israel, to play the harlot in her father's house. So you shall put away the evil from among you.

"If a man is found lying with a woman married to a husband, then both of them shall die — the man that lay with the woman, and the woman; so you shall put away the evil from Israel. "If a

young woman who is a virgin is betrothed to a husband, and a man finds her in the city and lies with her, then you shall bring them both out to the gate of that city, and you shall stone them to death with stones, the young woman because she did not cry out in the city, and the man because he humbled his neighbour's wife; so you shall put away the evil from among you. "But if a man finds a betrothed young woman in the countryside, and the man forces her and lies with her, then only the man who lay with her shall die. But you shall do nothing to the young woman; there is in the young woman no sin deserving of death, for just as when a man rises against his neighbour and kills him, even so is this matter. For he found her in the countryside, and the betrothed young woman cried out, but there was no one to save her. "If a man finds a young woman who is a virgin, who is not betrothed, and he seizes her and lies with her, and they are found out, then the man who lay with her shall give to the young woman's father fifty shekels of silver, and she shall be his wife because he has humbled her; he shall not be permitted to divorce her all his days. Deut 22:13-29

One can conclude that while women got serious punishments for indiscriminate sex, men only got severely punished when they committed adultery with a married woman and when they raped a woman. Instead of creating room for arguments, it is better to realise that there is protection in the law of God. The rules are not too hard for an average woman. If we could help our girls know early on that they are not missing out on anything by honouring God and that there is a time for everything, they will be fine.

Lot's Wife

As morning dawned, the angels urged Lot, saying, "Up! Take your wife and your two daughters who are here, lest you be swept away in the punishment of the city." But he lingered. So the men seized him and his wife and his two daughters by the hand, the Lord being merciful to him, and they brought him out and set him outside the city. And as they brought them out, one said, "Escape for your life. Do not look back or stop anywhere in the valley. Escape to the hills, lest you be swept away." And Lot said to them, "Oh, no, my lords. Behold, your servant has found favor in your sight, and you have shown me great kindness in saving my life. But I cannot escape to the hills, lest the disaster overtake me and I die. Behold, this city is near enough to flee to, and it is a little one. Let me escape there—is it not a little one?—and my life will be saved!" He said to him, "Behold, I grant you this favor also, that I will not overthrow the city of which you have spoken. Escape there quickly, for I can do nothing till you arrive there." Therefore the name of the city was called Zoar. The sun had risen on the earth when Lot came to Zoar. Then the Lord rained on Sodom and Gomorrah sulfur and fire from the Lord out of heaven. And he overthrew those cities, and all the valley, and all the inhabitants of the cities, and what grew on the ground. But Lot's wife, behind him, looked back, and she became a pillar of salt. Gen 19:15-26 ESV

Do not look back. The instruction was simple. When I was a child, the story of Lot's wife was one of the first bible stories I was taught. It was simply a story of obedience. In Luke 17. 32 our Lord Jesus Christ referred to it again.

During Sunday school, some teachers said she turned back because of her earthly belongings; they said she had a lot of jewelry and clothes and so she wasn't happy about leaving everything behind, thus she was greedy.

I think she probably turned out of sheer curiosity. Curiosity is the need to know what exactly is happening... The need to know what everyone is doing. To satisfy our inquisitiveness, we sometimes disregard instructions and put ourselves at risk. Curiosity can be a perilous emotion if we don't learn how to control it.

We must learn to trust the Lord and turn our backs on worldliness with all its appeal. Curiosity can make a man dwell on what he lost because he chose godliness. Looking at the wrong things can make you get anxious, depressed and discontented. People can still turn into a pillar of salt by looking back. I mean, they can get stagnated and never function the way they ought.

Daughters of Lot

So Lot went out and spoke to his sons-in-law, who had married his daughters, and said, "Get up, get out of this place; for the LORD will destroy this city!" But to his sons-in-law he seemed to be joking. When the morning dawned, the angels urged Lot to hurry, saying, "Arise, take your wife and your two daughters who are here, lest you be consumed in the punishment of the city." And while he lingered, the men took hold of his hand, his wife's hand, and the hands of his two daughters, the LORD being merciful to him, and they brought him out and set him outside the city. Gen.19.16-14

Lot and his daughters felt the pain of having sons-in-law/ husbands who are spiritually insensitive and ignorant. The danger of such inadequacy is that you keep trying to make up for their lack of spiritual understanding.

Marriage results in destiny merging, so it is very important that you think twice and pray before deciding on who you are merging your destiny with. Every decision your spouse makes affects you. It is always better to marry someone who believes the same things as you. Also, it is not smart to marry someone you cannot influence to do the right thing. Lot's sons-in-law could have followed him. They had nothing to lose by listening to him. If they respected him and regarded his person, they would have been able to see that all they had to do was go with him and if nothing like what he said was going to happen took place, then they could simply return.

Some people believed Lot had over two daughters and that the sons-in-law mentioned were not the husbands of the daughters in the house, because in subsequent verses, Lot referred to them as virgins. Whether those men were the husbands (or fiancé, as some also believed) of the daughters that Lot left Sodom and Gomorrah with or not, one thing was certain, they died even though they didn't have to. If truly they were married to another set of daughters, it means their insensitivity also cost the lives of their wives, and maybe children.

> *Then Lot went up out of Zoar and dwelt in the mountains, and his two daughters were with him; for he was afraid to dwell in Zoar. And he and his two daughters dwelt in a cave. Now the firstborn said to the younger, "Our father is old, and <u>there is no man on the earth to come in</u> to us as is the custom of all the earth. Come, let us make our father drink wine, and we will lie with him, that we may preserve the lineage of our father." So they made their father drink wine that night. And the firstborn went in and lay with her father, and he did not know when she lay down or when she arose. It happened on the next day that the firstborn said to the younger, "Indeed I lay with my father last night; let us make him drink wine tonight also, and you go in and lie with him, that we may preserve the lineage of our father."*

> *Then they made their father drink wine that night also. And the younger arose and lay with him, and he did not know when she lay down or when she arose. Thus both the daughters of Lot were with child by their father. The firstborn bore a son and*

called his name Moab; he is the father of the Moabites to this day. And the younger, she also bore a son and called his name Ben-Ammi; he is the father of the people of Ammon to this day. Gen.19.30-38

Women are ingenious. Women are bold. There is nothing a woman sets her mind to do that she cannot do -- nothing, regardless of whether it's a good or bad thing.

Several questions arose in my heart as I read their story - Incest? Desperation? Error? Preservation? Ignorance? Sin? The effects of alcohol?

Thinking about their actions, I wondered if the "unlawful deeds" they witnessed while living in Sodom and Gomorrah affected them more than they knew. Perhaps, after seeing sex being so trivialized, they probably didn't think it was a big deal. Their father, Lot, at some point, even offered them to the sodomites.

- See now, I have two daughters who have not known a man; please, let me bring them out to you, and you may do to them as you wish; only do nothing to these men, since this is the reason they have come under the shadow of my roof." Gen.19.8.

Perhaps, they were simply victims of living in a corrupt society where anything can be viewed as a solution to a problem, irrespective of its moral standards.

Some scholars believe that Lot's daughters thought the whole world had been destroyed and they were the only survivors left.

Perhaps that was why they resorted to sleeping with their father without his consent?

As I sat in my balcony, pondering, I couldn't help but think that if they had discussed the 'world' events with their father, they may have had a better understanding of what was going on. This points to the need for parents to have deep conversations with their children.

Lot, missing his wife and all he had lost, was probably just happy he got 2 grandsons from the bargain ... He probably never knew what his daughters did. Until he died, he probably never knew the boys he called grandsons were actually his sons.

Euodia and Syntyche

I urge Euodia and Syntyche to iron out their differences and make up. God doesn't want his children holding grudges. And, oh, yes, Syzygus, since you're right there to help them work things out, do your best with them. These women worked for the Message hand in hand with Clement and me, and with the other veterans — worked as hard as any of us. Remember, their names are also in the book of life. Phil 4:4-5 MESSAGE

Years ago, a certain nice woman said to me, "I don't want to get too committed in a church because I like to avoid drama...If I told you the things I saw when I tried to function in departments or serve in committees you would think I was exaggerating."

Disagreements are part of life; wherever you have people, there must be disagreements because of personal, ideological and theological differences. But, as we yield more to the power and love of God, disagreements become a thing of the past. Read, *"Remind them to be subject to rulers and authorities, to obey, to be ready for every good work, to speak evil of no one, to be peaceable, gentle, showing all humility to all men. For we ourselves were also once foolish, disobedient, deceived, serving various lusts and pleasures, living in malice and envy, hateful and hating one another. But when the kindness and the love of God our Saviour toward man appeared, not by works of righteousness which we have done, but according to His mercy He saved us, through the washing of regeneration and renewing of the Holy Spirit…* Titus 3:1-5

See what Apostle Paul said in the NLT *"Now I appeal to Euodia and Syntyche. Please, because you belong to the Lord, settle your disagreement."* He reminded them of their new position and encouraged them to settle their disagreement because in Christ there should be no place for personal agendas or power plays.

Apostle Paul then asked for intervention. He said, *"And I ask you, my true partner, to help these two women, for they worked hard with me in telling others the Good News."* Phil 4:3.

You may wonder why it was so important that they mend fences… it was so important because they risked losing the reward for all the good things they had done.

The bible said that wherever there is strife, there is evil work, quarrelling members are a big distraction to the church because unity is very important in the accomplishment of the divine commission. It is unwise to let yourself be an instrument in the enemy's hand… do not be a weapon of distraction. In Hebrews 12:1, we are admonished to lay aside every weight. This means dealing with character flaws because they get in the way and stop you from relating peaceably with others. Never be the reason someone is scared to serve in church; say no to party spirit, domineering control, and irrelevant confrontations.

Therefore, laying aside all malice, all deceit, hypocrisy, envy, and all evil speaking, as newborn babes, desire the pure milk of the word, that you may grow thereby, 1 Peter 2:1-2

In 1Cor 14:20 we are told, *"do not be children in understanding; however, in malice be babes, but in understanding be mature."*

When we focus on what is important, we wouldn't have deep disagreements and resentment. Here is what is important, *"Celebrate God all day, every day. I mean, revel in him! Make it as clear as you can to all you meet that you're on their side, working with them and not against them. Help them see that the Master is about to arrive. He could show up any minute!* Phil 4:4-5 MESSAGE

Bathsheba

One late afternoon, David got up from taking his nap and was strolling on the roof of the palace. From his vantage point on the roof he saw a woman bathing. The woman was stunningly beautiful. David sent to ask about her, and was told, "Isn't this Bathsheba, daughter of Eliam and wife of Uriah the Hittite?" David sent his agents to get her. After she arrived, he went to bed with her. (This occurred during the time of "purification" following her period.) Then she returned home. Before long she realized she was pregnant.

Later she sent word to David: "I'm pregnant." I sam 11:2-5

Bathsheba, the wife of Uriah, seems like a good example of a woman without strong values, a woman without a voice, without an opinion, without depth and without loyalty. Such women are great and easy to get along with until your life depends on them. Women like that don't plot anyone's downfall, yet will do nothing to stop anyone's destruction. They are just there, fancy packages, but never a force to reckon with. But could she have done anything?

David then got in touch with Joab. "Send Uriah the Hittite to me" Joab sent him. When he arrived, David asked him for news from the front — how things were going with Joab and the troops and with the fighting. Then he said to Uriah, "Go home. Have a refreshing bath and a good night rest". After Uriah left the palace, an informant of the king was sent after him. But Uriah didn't go home. He slept that night at the palace entrance, along with the king's servants. David was told that Uriah had not gone home. He asked Uriah, "Didn't you just come off a hard trip? So why didn't you go home"

Uriah replied to David, "The Chest is out there with the fighting men of Israel and Judah — in tents. My master Joab and his servants are roughing it out in the fields. So, how can I go home and eat and drink and enjoy my wife? On your life, I'll not do it!"

"All right," said David, "have it your way. Stay for the day and I'll send you back tomorrow." So Uriah stayed in Jerusalem the rest of the day.

The next day David invited him to eat and drink with him, and David got him drunk. But in the evening Uriah again went out and slept with his master's servants. He didn't go home. In the morning David wrote a letter to Joab and sent it with Uriah. In the letter he wrote, "Put Uriah in the front lines where the fighting is the fiercest. Then pull back and leave him exposed so that he's sure to be killed."

So Joab, holding the city under siege, put Uriah in a place where he knew there were fierce enemy fighters. When the city's defenders came out to fight Joab, some of David's soldiers were killed, including Uriah the Hittite.

Joab sent David a full report on the battle. He instructed the messenger, "After you have given to the king a detailed report on the battle, if he flares in anger, say, 'And by the way, your servant Uriah the Hittite is dead."

Joab's messenger arrived in Jerusalem and gave the king a full report. He said, "The enemy was too much for us. They advanced on us in the open field, and we pushed them back to the city gate. But then arrows came hot and heavy on us from the city wall, and eighteen of the king's soldiers died." When the messenger completed his report of the battle, David got angry at Joab. He vented it on the messenger: "Why did you get so close to the city? Didn't you know you'd be attacked from the wall? Didn't you remember how Abimelech son of Jerub-Besheth got killed? Wasn't it a woman who dropped a millstone on him from the wall and crushed him at Thebez? Why did you go close to the wall!"

"By the way," said Joab's messenger, "your servant Uriah the Hittite is dead."

Then David told the messenger, "Oh. I see. Tell Joab, 'Don't trouble yourself over this. War kills — sometimes one, sometimes another — you never know who's next. Redouble your assault on the city and destroy it.' Encourage Joab."

When Uriah's wife heard that her husband was dead, she grieved for her husband. When the time of mourning was over, David sent someone to bring her to his house. She became his wife and bore him a son. 2 Sam 11:6-27

Some scholars believe that Bathsheba was the granddaughter of Ahithophel because her father Eliam was the son of Ahithophel, David's wise counsellor.

> *"Is this not Bathsheba, the daughter of Eliam, the wife of Uriah the Hittite?"* 2 Sam 11:3-4

> *...Eliam the son of Ahithophel the Gilonite,* 2 Samuel 23:33

This could explain why Ahithophel later turned against David and counselled Absalom to publicly have sex with his father's concubines. And why he killed himself after his counsel to chase after and kill David was not taken by Absalom.

I didn't read anywhere that Bathsheba responded to any of the events around her or asked questions, and I don't think she could have been unaware of what happened. It is probably because women like Bathsheba don't stand or fight for anything really, they only answer to their names and live for themselves. Some women lack willpower and empathy. They prefer to act like a doormat than bother to ask penitent questions; exhibiting wisdom seems too much, they don't take sides either. They have a robotic tendency to do what they are told without thinking it through.

Women like that are hardly useful for matters of state and policy. Their key attribute is their physical beauty. They have stifled their conscience and hardly have a deep passion for anything or anyone. Right and wrong mean the same thing to them.

> *So Nathan spoke to Bathsheba the mother of Solomon, saying, "Have you not heard that Adonijah the son of Haggith has*

become king, and David our lord does not know it? Come, please, let me now give you advice, that you may save your own life and the life of your son Solomon. Go immediately to King David and say to him, 'Did you not, my lord, O king, swear to your maidservant, saying," Assuredly your son Solomon shall reign after me, and he shall sit on my throne"? Why then has Adonijah become king?' Then, while you are still talking there with the king, I also will come in after you and confirm your words."

So Bathsheba went into the chamber to the king. (Now the king was very old, and Abishag the Shunammite was serving the king). And Bathsheba bowed and did homage to the king. Then the king said, "What is your wish?" Then she said to him, "My lord, you swore by the Lord your God to your maidservant, saying, 'Assuredly Solomon your son shall reign after me, and he shall sit on my throne.' So now, look! Adonijah has become king; and now, my lord the king, you do not know about it. He has sacrificed oxen and fattened cattle and sheep in abundance, and has invited all the sons of the king, Abiathar the priest, and Joab the commander of the army; but Solomon your servant he has not invited. And as for you, my lord, O king, the eyes of all Israel are on you, that you should tell them who will sit on the throne of my lord the king after him Otherwise it will happen, when my lord the king rests with his fathers, that I and my son Solomon will be counted as offenders." 1 Kings 1:11-21NKJV

Bathsheba was a woman who could be easily influenced. She does well when she has a good counselor. As we saw in the scripture above, such women act when they are told to do so, but they don't think deeply enough to create any strategies or be discerning about issues.

"Ask King Solomon — he won't turn you down — to give me Abishag the Shunammite as my wife."

"Certainly," said Bathsheba. "I'll speak to the king for you."

Bathsheba went to King Solomon to present Adonijah's request. The king got up and welcomed her, bowing respectfully, and returned to his throne. Then he had a throne put in place for his mother, and she sat at his right hand. She said, "I have a small favor to ask of you. Don't refuse me." The king replied, "Go ahead, Mother; of course I won't refuse you." She said, "Give Abishag the Shunammite to your brother Adonijah as his wife."

King Solomon answered his mother, "What kind of favour is this, asking that Abishag the Shunammite be given to Adonijah? Why don't you just ask me to hand over the whole kingdom to him on a platter since he is my older brother and has Abiathar the priest and Joab son of Zeruiah on his side!"

Then King Solomon swore under God, "May God do his worst to me if Adonijah doesn't pay for this with his life! 24 As surely as God lives, the God who has set me firmly on the throne of my father David and has put me in charge of the kingdom just as he promised, Adonijah will die for this — today!" 1 Kings 2:17-24

Don't ask a Bathsheba for counsel, she hardly has an opinion about things. She just lives and watches everything else unfold.

Abigail

Abigail was the wife of Nabal. She later became David's wife.

"Meanwhile, one of the young shepherds told Abigail, Nabal's wife, what had happened: "David sent messengers from the backcountry to salute our master, but he tore into them with insults. Yet these men treated us very well. They took nothing from us and didn't take advantage of us all the time we were in the fields. They formed a wall around us, protecting us day and night all the time we were out tending the sheep. Do something quickly because big trouble is ahead for our master and all of us. Nobody can talk to him. He's impossible — a real brute!"

Abigail flew into action. She took two hundred loaves of bread, two skins of wine, five sheep dressed out and ready for cooking, a bushel of roasted grain, a hundred raisin cakes, and two hundred fig cakes, and she had it all loaded on some donkeys. Then she said to her young servants, "Go ahead and pave the way for me. I'm right behind you." But she said nothing to her husband Nabal.

As she was riding her donkey, descending into a ravine, David and his men were descending from the other end, so they met there on the road. David had just said, "That sure was a waste, guarding everything this man had out in the wild so that nothing he had was lost — and now he rewards me with insults. A real slap in the face! May God do his worst to me if Nabal and every

*cur in his misbegotten brood isn't dead meat by morning!"*1 Sam 25
14-22

One of the most troublesome questions I get asked is, "What can someone do when they marry wrong?" What is next after you realise your spouse is a terrible person; a wicked or a violent man? A rapist? Philanderer? Drug addict? Pedophile? Squanderer? etc" I never have a general answer to that question because there isn't any; we only get to gain clarity after personal sessions where the details are known. I have seen abusive people repent. I have seen alcoholics and gamblers change. I have also seen where they didn't and it seemed like all the hope and sacrifices of their partners were in vain. The strength of character is not determined by how much wickedness you can endure. So, prayer is very important because only God can help you know what steps you need to take.

Being a supportive wife does not mean endorsing foolishness or abandoning your God-given grace and ability to discern and do what is right. If your husband habitually does the wrong things; acts wickedly or stupidly, you have a moral obligation to talk to him and not support his wrong actions. Every man can renew his mind and change. I always say being male does not rob anyone of the ability to be decent, kind, sensitive, loving and temperate.

If your man makes a mistake, let him repent and grow. If he offends someone, loyalty does not mean ignoring/supporting his wrong deed and fighting the innocent with him. No, rather pray for him, talk to him in a way he can understand, encourage him to be good. If you love him, you will inspire him to be a better person.

Sapphira

Sapphira was the wife of Ananias. They were the duo that were struck dead because they lied about the price they sold their piece of land for.

But a certain man named Ananias, with Sapphira his wife, sold a possession. And he kept back part of the proceeds, his wife also being aware of it, and brought a certain part and laid it at the apostles' feet. But Peter said, "Ananias, why has Satan filled your heart to lie to the Holy Spirit and keep back part of the price of the land for yourself? While it remained, was it not your own? And after it was sold, was it not in your own control? Why have you conceived this thing in your heart? You have not lied to men but to God."

Then Ananias, hearing these words, fell down and breathed his last. So great fear came upon all those who heard these things. And the young men arose and wrapped him up, carried him out, and buried him. Now it was about three hours later when his wife came in, not knowing what had happened. And Peter answered her, "Tell me whether you sold the land for so much?"

She said, "Yes, for so much."

Then Peter said to her, "How is it that you have agreed together to test the Spirit of the Lord? Look, the feet of those who have buried your husband are at the door, and they will carry you out." Then immediately she fell down at his feet and breathed her last. And the young men came in and found her dead, and carrying her out, buried her by her husband. Acts 5:1-10

Have you ever met people who want you to feel like they are doing more than they are? Just because they want you to feel obligated, intimidated and grateful for any little deed, they tend to over-emphasise and hype it. Ananias and Sapphira didn't have to lie about the price of the land. It is better to say "Pastor, we sold the land for S1000and we want to give S500". Instead of lying that you sold the land for S500 and you are giving everything to God.

Sapphira was an accomplice to unrighteousness. Some people do stupid things in pursuit of the praise and validation of men. In our service to God, we should never forget that our service is to God; God sees everything and He cannot be mocked. In today's congregations, some still act like Sapphira, they falsify records and exaggerate results. I find all those exaggerations unnecessary. Dare to be different, be truthful, even if the structure encourages exaggeration. If you get everyone to think you have sacrificed everything when you haven't, you have deceived yourself. The only true report card is with the Father; aim to please Him and never forget he knows you well. Never forget, He is the just judge and righteous God.

The Shunammite Woman

Wisdom... Kindness... Faith... Reward

Now it happened one day that Elisha went to Shunem, where there was a notable woman, and she persuaded him to eat some food. So it was, as often as he passed by, he would turn in there to eat some food. And she said to her husband, "Look now, I know that this is a holy man of God, who passes by us regularly. Please, let us make a small upper room on the wall; and let us put a bed for him there, and a table and a chair and a lampstand; so it will be, whenever he comes to us, he can turn in there." 2 Kings 4:8-10

The Shunammite woman was a kind and sensitive woman. She first provided food for Elisha, then recognised the man of God would need decent accommodation, and she spoke to her husband about it. So, they made a comfortable lodging for the man of God without him asking them. To do good without being obliged is genuine kindness.

One day when Elisha came, he went up to his room and lay down there. He said to his servant Gehazi, "Call the Shunammite." So he called her, and she stood before him. Elisha said to him, "Tell her, 'You have gone to all this trouble for us.

193

Now what can be done for you? Can we speak on your behalf to the king or the commander of the army?"

She replied, "I have a home among my own people."

"What can be done for her?" Elisha asked.

Gehazi said, "Well, she has no son and her husband is old."

Then Elisha said, "Call her." So he called her, and she stood in the doorway. "About this time next year," Elisha said, "you will hold a son in your arms."

"No, my lord," she objected. "Don't mislead your servant, O man of God!" But the woman became pregnant, and the next year about that same time she gave birth to a son, just as Elisha had told her. 2 Kings 4:11-17 NIV

Doing good is showing faith. When we do good, we open doors of blessings and attract favours even without asking for them. The Shunammite woman just wanted to help. She wasn't sowing those seeds of honour because she had a need. The Shunammite woman saw helping the Prophet Elisha as a privilege and an opportunity to serve God.

Several times I have been opportune to meet people like the Shunammite woman. I sometimes lay prostrate on the floor, thanking God for them. They do so much good with no strings attached... one of them said, "Blessing you give me joy". Another said, "God wants me to do it. I know because the way I feel excited about it is so deep".

I smiled because I understood. As a missionary, there were times when I talked to God about my finances. And so if I walked into a store and someone walked up to me and insisted on paying, I knew it was God's answer. But I appreciate givers so much because I know it is not everyone God talks to that responds. Some people are comfortably sitting on others' blessings. I have met several people who said God told them to help someone, and they procrastinated or never did. I never want to be the person who refuses to extend a hand of blessing when God has nudged me.

When my husband and I were planning for our wedding, God even used total strangers to bless us. It was mind-blowing. To be used by God to bless others is the best feeling ever and more so when they are His servants; it is one of the greatest blessings ever because God rewards beautifully.

Our kind deeds attract pleasantness to us. The Shunammite became a candidate for divine upliftment the moment she became a blessing to God's servant. Whether she had faith to conceive was immaterial, her good seeds had singled her out to receive the blessing of "fullness of joy." The blessing of "fullness of Joy" is a blessing that seeks to add completeness. It chases you down, finds any area where you need divine enablement and then supplies it. **This blessing preserves.**

> *When the child was old enough, he went out one day to be with his father, who was with the reapers. Suddenly he cried out to his father, "My head! My head hurts!" He said to his servant, "Carry him back to his mother." When he had taken him and brought him to his mother, he lay on her lap until noon; and then*

he died. She went up and laid him on the bed of the man of God, shut the door on him and went out. She called to her husband and said, "Please send me one of the servants with a donkey. I must get to the man of God as fast as I can; I'll come straight back."

*He asked, "Why are you going to him today? It isn't Rosh-Hodesh and it isn't Shabbat." She said, "It's all right." Then she saddled the donkey and ordered her servant, "Drive as fast as you can; don't slow down for me unless I say so."*2 Kings 4:18-24 CJB

As she approached the man of God at Mount Carmel, Elisha saw her in the distance. He said to Gehazi, "Look, the woman from Shunem is coming. Run out to meet her and ask her, 'Is everything all right with you, your husband, and your child?"

"Yes," the woman told Gehazi, "everything is fine."

But when she came to the man of God at the mountain, she fell to the ground before him and caught hold of his feet. Gehazi began to push her away, but the man of God said, "Leave her alone. She is deeply troubled, but the Lord has not told me what it is." Then she said, "Did I ask you for a son, my lord? And didn't I say, 'Don't deceive me and get my hopes up'?"

Then Elisha said to Gehazi, "Get ready to travel; take my staff and go! Don't talk to anyone along the way. Go quickly and lay the staff on the child's face." But the boy's mother said, "As surely as the Lord lives and you yourself live, I won't go home unless you go with me." So Elisha returned with her.

Gehazi hurried on ahead and laid the staff on the child's face, but nothing happened. There was no sign of life. He returned to meet Elisha and told him, "The child is still dead."

When Elisha arrived, the child was indeed dead, lying there on the prophet's bed. He went in alone and shut the door behind him and prayed to the Lord. Then he lay down on the child's body, placing his mouth on the child's mouth, his eyes on the child's eyes, and his hands on the child's hands. And as he stretched out on him, the child's body began to grow warm again! Elisha got up, walked back and forth across the room once, and then stretched himself out again on the child. This time the boy sneezed seven times and opened his eyes!

Then Elisha summoned Gehazi. "Call the child's mother!" he said. And when she came in, Elisha said, "Here, take your son!" She fell at his feet and bowed before him, overwhelmed with gratitude. Then she took her son in her arms and carried him downstairs. 2 Kings 4:25-37

The Widow of Zarephath

Elijah obeyed God's orders. He went and camped in the Kerith canyon on the other side of the Jordan. And sure enough, ravens brought him his meals, both breakfast and supper, and he drank from the brook. Eventually, the brook dried up because of the drought. Then God spoke to him: "Get up and go to Zarephath in Sidon and live there. I've instructed a woman who lives there, a widow, to feed you." So he got up and went to Zarephath. As he came to the entrance of the village, he met a woman, a widow, gathering firewood. He asked her, "Please, would you bring me a little water in a jug? I need a drink." As she went to get it, he called out, "And while you're at it, would you bring me something to eat?"

She said, "I swear, as surely as your God lives, I don't have so much as a biscuit. I have a handful of flour in a jar and a little oil in a bottle; you found me scratching together just enough firewood to make a last meal for my son and me. After we eat it, we'll die." 1 Kings 17:5-12

We sometimes want everything to be ready. As a pastor, you expect everyone to serve, especially when God already told you about them, but that is not always the case. Sometimes, even after God has instructed people through direct visions, they still need help to step into their roles. The woman of Zarephath didn't seem surprised at Elijah's request rather, she seemed prepared to resist. Chances are that the thought of bringing a cake along with the water had already crossed her mind, and she shrugged it off with, "if only I had enough, I would have loved to bless this man of God".

God cannot lie. If things look different from what God told you, know that the variation is from the human side. And use your faith to bring God's Word to pass. Elijah did just that. In today's world, some may have misunderstood Elijah or felt like he was being unfair to the widow. But carnal reasoning cannot understand faith. The fact that charlatans have abused this principle does not make it ineffective. As a preacher in this dispensation of false prophets and a high rate of extorted and hurt people, telling people how much God can bless them for kind service is not always easy. But we must teach the whole counsel of God's Word; God loves it when people give. God wants you to give whenever He instructs you to. And He blesses you abundantly for it. Every time there is an opportunity to give see it as a sign that God wants to give you a miracle.

Elijah said to her, "Don't worry about a thing. Go ahead and do what you've said. But first make a small biscuit for me and bring it back here. Then go ahead and make a meal from what's left for you and your son. This is the word of the God of Israel: 'The jar of flour will not run out and the bottle of oil will not become empty before God sends rain on the land and ends this drought." And she went right off and did it, did just as Elijah asked. And it turned out as he said — daily food for her and her family. The jar of meal didn't run out and the bottle of oil didn't become empty: God's promise fulfilled to the letter, exactly as Elijah had delivered it! 1 Kings 17:13-16 MESSAGE

Some people have short memories when recounting the blessings of God and His mighty interventions.

> *Sometime later, the woman's son became sick. He grew worse and worse, and finally he died. Then she said to Elijah, "O man of God, what have you done to me? Have you come here to point out my sins and kill my son?"*

The widow of Zarephath forgot that the God who provided food for her household and stopped them from dying of hunger cares about her. She remembered her sins, but she forgot His grace. She suspected Elijah. I praise the Lord for hearing Elijah, I don't want to think about what may have happened to Elijah if the boy wasn't resurrected; an angry mob might have lynched him over something he knew nothing of. Thank God for miracles. We need the power of God to do the Work of God.

> *But Elijah replied, "Give me your son." And he took the child's body from her arms, carried him up the stairs to the room where he was staying, and laid the body on his bed. Then Elijah cried out to the Lord, "O Lord my God, why have you brought tragedy to this widow who has opened her home to me, causing her son to die?" And he stretched himself out over the child three times and cried out to the Lord, "O Lord my God, please let this child's life return to him." The Lord heard Elijah's prayer, and the life of the child returned, and he revived! Then Elijah brought him down from the upper room and gave him to his mother. "Look!" he said. "Your son is alive!" Then the woman told Elijah, "Now I know for sure that you are a man of God, and that the Lord truly speaks through you."* 1 Kings 17:17-24

In verse 24, she finally realised she was not dealing with an ordinary man and declared so. I thank God for His mercy; He is not quick to anger. He loves us so much. He saves us from ourselves. He understands and pities our shortcomings and helps us despite all.

Caleb's Daughter

Then Caleb said, "Whoever attacks Kirjath Sepher and takes it, to him I will give my daughter Achsah as wife." And Othniel the son of Kenaz, Caleb's younger brother, took it; so he gave him his daughter Achsah as wife. Now it happened, when she came to him, that she urged him to ask her father for a field. And she dismounted from her donkey, and Caleb said to her, "What do you wish?" So she said to him,"Give me a blessing; since you have given me land in the South, give me also springs of water."

And Caleb gave her the upper springs and the lower springs.
Judg 1:12-15 NKJV

Caleb's daughter was audacious. Talk about boldness, wisdom and faith. Caleb's daughter expressed all three. Many people are living below their potential because they won't ask for what they need. Some are suffering needlessly because they are afraid.

For example, your dad gets you a car while you are schooling but forgets to increase your upkeep allowance with money for fuel. First, you are grateful for the car, but you can't drive the car without fuel. You know he can provide for it and he doesn't what you to work while schooling. Should you talk to him about it or whine and complain? Or just pack the car and never use it?

Caleb's daughter had been given a piece of land, but she needed water to make the land useful to her... would asking for water be too much?

Ask for what you want, you can only either get a yes or no. It is better to ask and be denied than to be silent, because, then you will never if you would have got a yes.

Everyone on earth had needed a little help; a break, a concession, some advantage, some favour —whatever you may call it...we have all, at some point, needed something someone else had to give. So, never be scared to say what you need but always maintain a good attitude whatever the outcome.

The Matriarchs

Mothers are matriarchs. They are like the glue that holds everything together. They are like a compass that determines the direction.

> *The wise woman builds her house,*
> *But the foolish pulls it down with her hands.* Prov 14:1

Then God caused a deep sleep to fall upon the person; and while he was sleeping, he took one of his ribs and closed up the place from which he took it with flesh. The rib which Adonai, God, had taken from the person, he made a woman-person; and he brought her to the man-person. The man-person said, "At last! This is bone from my bones and flesh from my flesh. She is to be called Woman [Hebrew: ishah], because she was taken out of Man [Hebrew: ish]." Gen 2:21-24 CJB

The man called his wife Havah [life], because she was the mother of all living. Gen 3:20 CJB

In the CJB- Complete Jewish Bible, Eve is called Havah (meaning life). Eve was the first woman created, the wife of Adam, the mother of Cain, Abel and Seth.

Now the serpent was more crafty than any wild animal which Adonai, God, had made. He said to the woman, "Did God really say, 'You are not to eat from any tree in the garden'?" The woman answered the serpent, "We may eat from the fruit of the trees of the garden, but about the fruit of the tree in the middle of the garden God said, 'You are neither to eat from it nor touch it, or you will die." The serpent said to the woman, "It is not true that you will surely die; because God knows that on the day you eat from it, your eyes will be opened, and you will be like God, knowing good and evil." When the woman saw that the tree was good for food, that it had a pleasing appearance and that the tree was desirable for making one wise, she took some of its fruit and ate. She also gave some to her husband, who was with her; and he ate. Gen 3:1-7 CJB

Some ask if Eve was really disobedient, since she was not directly warned against eating the fruit. We may not have read where God told her not to eat the fruit, but we know from the conversation that ensued that she was aware.

Adonai, God, called to the man, "Where are you?" He answered, "I heard your voice in the garden, and I was afraid, because I was naked, so I hid myself." He said, "Who told you that you were naked? Have you eaten from the tree from which I ordered you not to eat?" The man replied, "The woman you gave to be with me — she gave me fruit from the tree, and I ate." Adonai, God, said to the woman, "What is this you have done?" The woman answered, "The serpent tricked me, so I ate." Gen 3:9-13 CJB.

Eve reminds us of the danger of disobedience. Disobedience precedes a fall from grace. Hate it or like it. Blessings always come with a demand for obedience. Eve reminds us that disobedience is birthed whenever we deviate from the Master plan; deviation arises because of temptation. Temptation comes when the enemy uses our ambitious desire as bait.

To the woman he said, "I will greatly increase your pain in childbirth. You will bring forth children in pain. <u>Your desire will be toward your husband, but he will rule over you.</u>" To Adam he said, "Because you listened to what your wife said and ate from the tree about which I gave you the order, 'You are not to eat *from it,' the ground is cursed on your account; you will work hard to eat from it as long as you live.* Gen 3:16-17 CJB

Always pray and make consultations with God before taking any steps. If our need to have more and be more is leading us towards rebellion, we should know that is a wrong step. Any step towards supposedly "more progress", that leads us away from God is retrogression in disguise. Any place where ambition becomes a vice and not virtue is not a good place.

We ought to practise and master being content. Now, this is sensitive, because some folks think being content means being complacent, but they are very different.

From the underlined judgement God pronounced on Eve, we can tell that if being subservient to the man was a punishment for Eve's disobedience, then it proves that initially woman was not made to be subservient to man. Woman, the way God intended, before the fall, was a power-house. Are you still wondering why Christian women are breaking limits and bringing so much glory to God? It is because we have been redeemed in Christ, we have learned to be wiser and humble from Eve's story. We are walking in new creation realities and we have learned how to manage our power. Any woman, though, who abuses the authority of God and her husband's new creation realities or not, is setting herself up for a fall.

Studying Eve's account in the bible makes me humble; I thank God again for this book **"WOMEN OF LIFE"** and I besiege you to help us ensure it gets to virtually every woman and even man. Eve's account shows us again the power and influence of women.

Women are so pivotal in the scheme of things. The world will be a better place if we have more first ladies that are God-fearing. Godly women in leadership, and every other role (as wives and mothers), do amazing things.

Sarah

Sarah was the wife of Abraham and the mother of Isaac.

And God said unto Abraham, As for Sarai thy wife, thou shall not call her name Sarai, but Sarah shall her name be. And I will bless her, and give thee a son also of her: yea, I will bless her, and she shall be a mother of nations; kings of people shall be of her. Then Abraham fell upon his face, and laughed, and said in his heart, Shall a child be born unto him that is an hundred years old? and shall Sarah, that is ninety years old, bear? And Abraham said unto God, O that Ishmael might live before thee! And God said, Sarah thy wife shall bear thee a son indeed; and thou shall call his name Isaac: and I will establish my covenant with him for an everlasting covenant, and with his seed after him." Gen 17:15-19

Sarah was the wife of Abraham. She was so beautiful that her husband asked her to lie about their relationship to everyone who asked.

Now there was a famine in the land, and Abram went down to Egypt to dwell there, for the famine was severe in the land. And it came to pass, when he was close to entering Egypt, that he said to Sarai his wife, "Indeed I know that you are a woman of beautiful *countenance. Therefore it will happen, when the Egyptians see you, that they will say, 'This is his wife'; and they will kill me, but they will let you live. Please say you are my sister, that it may be well with me for your sake, and that I may live because of you." So it was, when Abram came into Egypt, that the Egyptians saw the woman, that she was very beautiful. The princes of Pharaoh also saw her and commended her to Pharaoh. And the woman was taken to Pharaoh's house.* He treated Abram well for her sake. He had sheep, oxen, male donkeys, male and female servants, female donkeys, and camels. But the Lord plagued Pharaoh and his house with great plagues because of Sarai, Abram's wife. And Pharaoh called Abram and said," What is this you have done to me? Why did you not tell me that she was your wife? Why did you say, 'She is my sister'? I might have taken her as my wife. Now therefore, here is your wife; take her and go your way." So Pharaoh commanded his men concerning him; and they sent him away, with his wife and all that he had.* Gen 12:10-20

"And yet indeed she is my sister; she is the daughter of my father, but not the daughter of my mother and she became my wife." Gen 20:12

Sarah was called Sarai until God changed her name to Sarah.

So Abraham hurried into the tent to Sarah and said, "Quickly, make ready three measures of fine meal; knead it and make cakes." And Abraham ran to the herd, took a tender and good calf, gave it to a young man, and he hastened to prepare it. 8 So he took butter and milk and the calf which he had prepared, and set it before them; and he stood by them under the tree as they ate. Then they said to him, "Where is Sarah your wife?"

So he said, "Here, in the tent."

And He said, "I will certainly return to you according to the time of life, and behold, Sarah your wife shall have a son.(Sarah was listening in the tent door which was behind him.) Now Abraham and Sarah were old, well advanced in age; and Sarah had passed the age of childbearing. Therefore Sarah laughed within herself, saying, "After I have grown old, shall I have pleasure, my lord being old also?" And the Lord said to Abraham, "Why did Sarah laugh, saying, 'Shall I surely bear a child, since I am old?' Is anything too hard for the Lord? At the appointed time I will return to you, according to the time of life, and Sarah shall have a son."

But Sarah denied it, saying, "I did not laugh," for she was afraid.And He said, "No, but you did laugh!" Gen 18:6-15

There are so many things to learn from Sarah's life.

Sarah helps us understand the dilemma of a woman struggling with conceiving and the desperation that comes from childlessness that can lead to poor judgments. Some women drink unbelievable concoctions, sought after solutions in strange places, encourage their husbands to cheat and sometimes even compromise their virtue themselves by cheating just to have a child.

Sarah's need and desperation led her to give Hagar her maid to Abraham, her husband, to sleep with so that she may have a child by her.

When Sarah saw that her plan, just like any plan outside of God's design, did not end well, she turned to God and settled His Word in her heart. You may ask how I know this. See Heb 11:11

."Through faith also Sarah herself received strength to conceive seed, and was delivered of a child when she was past age, because she judged him faithful who had promised."

Through faith, Sarah herself received the strength to conceive. Truth is, the best thing in every situation is to hold on to God, take His promise to the bank and cash out. Even though Sarah laughed when she heard she would be a mother, she still acted her faith by having sex with her husband. Remember her initial response, -*So Sarah laughed to herself, thinking, "I am old, and so is my lord; am I to have pleasure again?"* Gen 18:12-13CJB. Sex at that age was probably something she had expelled from her schedule.

Sarah is a woman of faith. Her moment of desperation did not rob her of that title. That you feel helpless or vulnerable does not mean you can't still build on your faith. So, forget your moments of doubt, your mistakes, your faithlessness and hold on to God's love.

Stand by His promise, and from henceforth cast your cares upon Him. Seek to know Him, and trust Him completely. *"He that cometh to God must believe that He is, and that He is a rewarder..."* Heb 11:5. Sarah had a testimony; God blessed her with a son whom she named Isaac, meaning *laughter*. Hallelujah! She came to a point where she settled God's word in her heart. She believed the one who made a promise would do what He said.

Looking at Sarah and Hagar's relationship, Sarah is a powerful woman who refused to be subjected to disrespect even though she gave room for it; she refused to pay for her error in judgment. I view Sarah as a queen or a CEO who did what she thought was right, and when it seemed she had promoted the wrong person, she refused to hold a pity party sulking, instead acted swiftly to bring the situation under control.

Sarah was blessed with a faithful spouse. When she reported the situation with Hagar to Abraham, he asked her to do as she deemed fit. She and her husband had a good relationship. It seemed there was nothing they couldn't talk about. I pray more couples will take advantage of the power of communication.

I have maximum respect for Sarah; she is the kind of woman that does what she needs to do. Remember, when she needed to say she was her husband's sister, she did, twice, without thinking twice. When she wanted a baby, she had to have one, even if through surrogacy. When surrogacy went wrong, she moved.

Hagar and Sarah's story shows us that strategies fail, and strong-will as beautiful as it is, is not all that is required to birth a miracle. It takes God, not men, to make your life perfect. Only God, thus, we will save ourselves a lot of heartaches if we choose to trust Him early.

Miriam

Then <u>Miriam the prophetess</u>, Aaron's sister, took a tambourine in her hand, <u>and all the women followed her</u>, with tambourines and dancing. <u>Miriam sang to them</u>:

> *"Sing to the Lord, for he is highly exalted.*
> *The horse and its rider he has hurled into the sea."* Ex 15:20-21 NIV

Miriam was a prophetess, a women's leader and a singer. On a certain day, I met someone, and she said, "If I had all the graces you have, hmmm nobody could talk to me, I would be all over the place lording it over people". Before I could reply, her friend responded and said, "God knows why He made you the way He did. . . so pride won't cause you to self-destruct". We all laughed about it and went our separate ways. But I thought about it again and thanked God for the grace of humility.

What would you do with a little more power? Would you disdain authority and disregard boundaries? Does glory make you loud? Should grace make you proud?

Never get carried away by self-exaltation.

Miriam and Aaron began to talk against Moses because of his Cushite wife, for he had married a Cushite. "Has the Lord spoken only through Moses?" they asked. "Hasn't he also spoken through

214

us?" And the Lord heard this. (Now Moses was a very humble man, more humble than anyone else on the face of the earth.) Num 12:1-3

Miriam and Aaron probably thought Moses was their equal or junior because of his humility; sometimes people think if you are not bragging and flaunting it is because you have nothing to brag about. Sometimes meekness is mistaken for weakness. Whenever you are misunderstood like this, do not rush to defend yourself or prove your value. Be patient, God will vindicate you. He always does.

At once, the Lord said to Moses, Aaron and Miriam, "Come out to the Tent of Meeting, all three of you." So the three of them came out. Then the Lord came down in a pillar of cloud; he stood at the entrance to the Tent and summoned Aaron and Miriam. When both of them stepped forward, he said,

Listen carefully to what I'm telling you.
If there is a prophet of God among you,
I make myself known to him in visions,
I speak to him in dreams.
But I don't do it that way with my servant Moses;
he has the run of my entire house;
I speak to him intimately, in person,
in plain talk without riddles:
He ponders the very form of God.
So why did you show no reverence or respect in speaking against my servant, against Moses?

The anger of God blazed out against them. And then he left. When the Cloud moved off from the Tent, oh! Miriam had turned leprous, her skin like snow. Aaron took one look at Miriam — a leper! He said to Moses, "Please, my master, please don't come down so hard on us for this foolish and thoughtless sin. Please don't make her like a stillborn baby coming out of its mother's womb with half its body decomposed."

The same Moses she disrespected prayed for her restoration because she could not have done it herself. God relates to everyone, yes, but they reveal His Grace in varying dimensions. Learn to humbly acknowledge your relationship with God without challenging another's because you can't tell how special they are to God. What are you using to judge- is it the size of the congregation, their age, the number of cars or television stations? You could be wrong? But being humble and loving is always right. So, celebrate and respect God's children. Let God exalt you before you exalt yourself, and when He does, remember it is for His glory.

And Moses prayed to God:
Please, God, heal her, please heal her. God answered Moses," If her father had spat in her face, wouldn't she be ostracized for seven days? Quarantine her outside the camp for seven days. Then she can be readmitted to the camp." So Miriam was in quarantine outside the camp for seven days. The people didn't march on until she was readmitted.
Num 12:6-15 Message

Rachael and Leah

Leah and Rachael are the two daughters of Laban, the brother of Rebecca and uncle to Jacob. They are the wives of Jacob.

And it came to pass, when Jacob saw Rachel the daughter of Laban his mother's brother, and the sheep of Laban his mother's brother, that Jacob went near and rolled the stone from the well's mouth, and watered the flock of Laban his mother's brother. Then Jacob kissed Rachel and lifted up his voice and wept. And Jacob told Rachel that he was her father's relative and that he was Rebekah's son. So she ran and told her father. Then it came to pass, when Laban heard the report about Jacob his sister's son, that he ran to meet him, and embraced him and kissed him, and brought him to his house. So he told Laban all these things. And Laban said to him, "Surely you are my bone and my flesh." And he stayed with him for a month.

Then Laban said to Jacob, "Because you are my relative, should you therefore serve me for nothing? Tell me, what should your wages be?" Now Laban had two daughters: the name of the elder was Leah, and the name of the younger was Rachel. Leah's eyes were delicate, but Rachel was beautiful of form and appearance. Now Jacob loved Rachel; so he said," I will serve you seven years for Rachel your younger daughter." And Laban said, "It is better that I give her to you than that I should give her to another man. Stay with me." So Jacob served seven years for Rachel, and they seemed only a few days to him because of the love he had for her. Gen 29:15-20

Then Jacob said to Laban, "Give me my wife; I've completed what we agreed I'd do. I'm ready to consummate my marriage." Laban invited everyone around and threw a big feast. At evening, though, he got his daughter Leah and brought her to the marriage bed, and Jacob slept with her. (Laban gave his maid Zilpah to his daughter Leah as her maid.)

Morning came: There was Leah in the marriage bed! Jacob confronted Laban, "What have you done to me? Didn't I work all this time for the hand of Rachel? Why did you cheat me?"

"We don't do it that way in our country," said Laban. "We don't marry off the younger daughter before the older. Enjoy your week of honeymoon, and then we'll give you the other one also. But it will cost you another seven years of work."

Jacob agreed. When he'd completed the honeymoon week, Laban gave him his daughter Rachel to be his wife. (Laban gave his maid Bilhah to his daughter Rachel as her maid.) Jacob then slept with her. And he loved Rachel more than Leah. He worked for Laban another seven years. Gen 29:21-30 THE MESSAGE.

We saw from the scriptures how Jacob became a husband of two sisters, even though he didn't plan to. Jacob fell in love with Rachael at first sight, probably because of her ingenuity and beauty. On their first encounter, Rachael was tending to her father's sheep. Now that is worthy of note. She was a female shepherd. There is something extra attractive about a woman who can pull her own weight.

Verse 16-17, said Leah was Tender eyed, but Rachael was beautiful and well-favoured.

Rachel was a beautiful young girl who had her dream life altered on the altar of tradition. Rachel had a strong character.

Leah was a woman that had to fight for her husband's love throughout her marriage. He didn't love her, and she knew it.

When the Lord saw that Leah was not loved, he opened her womb, but Rachel was barren. Leah became pregnant and gave birth to a son. She named him Reuben, for she said, "It is because the Lord has seen my misery. Surely my husband will love me now." She conceived again, and when she gave birth to a son she said, "Because the Lord heard that I am not loved, he gave me this one too." So she named him Simeon. Again she conceived, and when she gave birth to a son she said, "Now at last my husband will become attached to me, because I have borne him three sons." So he was named Levi. She conceived again, and when she gave birth to a son she said, "This time I will praise the Lord." So she named him Judah. Then she stopped having children. Gen 29:31-35 NIV

The dynamics between the two sisters were strange.

Should Leah have married Jacob, knowing full well that he had been working for her father for her sister Rachael's hand in marriage?

Or, even though Rachael had been preparing to marry Jacob because she knew he loved her and wanted to marry her, should Rachael had married Jacob after her father had given Leah to him?

Perhaps Leah thought she should not because she said to her, *"Is it a small matter that you have taken away my husband? Would you take away my son's mandrakes also?"* Gen 30:15 NKJV

Who do you think took away the other's husband? Who was the real husband snatcher? I don't know, but I celebrate them for being matriarchs. There is so much to learn from their lives.

Another strange twist is found in the way they gave their maids to Jacob. Rachael did it first because she had no child, and Leah did it because of rivalry. She wanted more children too; she felt her sons were her only edge over Rachael. Her children were her compensation, and she was not about to lose that advantage, in no way. From the way she named her sons, you can tell she was insecure in her marriage.

> *Now when Rachel saw that she bore Jacob no children, Rachel envied her sister, and said to Jacob, "Give me children, or else I die!"*
>
> *And Jacob's anger was aroused against Rachel, and he said,*
>
> *"Am I in the place of God, who has withheld from you the fruit of the womb?"*
>
> *So, she said, "Here is my maid Bilhah; go in to her, and she will bear a child on my knees, that I also may have children by her." Then she gave him Bilhah her maid as wife, and Jacob*

went in to her. And Bilhah conceived and bore Jacob a son. Then Rachel said, "God has judged my case; and He has also heard my voice and given me a son." Therefore she called his name Dan. And Rachel's maid Bilhah conceived again and bore Jacob a second son. Then Rachel said, <u>"With great wrestlings I have wrestled with my sister, and indeed I have prevailed.</u>" So she called his name Naphtali. Gen 30:1-8 NKJV

I applaud Rachel, though, for making the best of her situation. The rivalry didn't end here, though. Leah was not ready to let Rachel have the last laugh.

When Leah saw that she had stopped bearing, she took Zilpah her maid and gave her to Jacob as wife. And Leah's maid Zilpah bore Jacob a son. Then Leah said, "A troop comes!" So she called his name Gad. And Leah's maid Zilpah bore Jacob a second son. Then Leah said, "I am happy, for the daughters will call me blessed." So she called his name Asher.

Now Reuben went in the days of wheat harvest and found mandrakes in the field, and brought them to his mother Leah. Then Rachel said to Leah,<u>" Please give me some of your son's mandrakes." But she said to her,"Is it a small matter that you have taken away my husband? Would you take away my son's mandrakes also?"</u>

And Rachel said, "Therefore he will lie with you tonight for your son's mandrakes."

Rachel sure had a powerful influence over their husband.

When Jacob came out of the field in the evening, Leah went out to meet him and said, "You must come in to me, for I have surely hired you with my son's mandrakes." And he lay with her that night. And God listened to Leah, and she conceived and bore Jacob a fifth son. Leah said, "God has given me my wages, because I have given my maid to my husband." So she called his name Issachar. Then Leah conceived again and bore Jacob a sixth son. And Leah said, "God has endowed me with a good endowment; now my husband will dwell with me, because I have borne him six sons." So she called his name Zebulun. Afterward she bore a daughter, and called her name Dinah.

Then God remembered Rachel, and God listened to her and opened her womb. And she conceived and bore a son, and said, "God has taken away my reproach." So she called his name Joseph, and said, "The Lord shall add to me another son." Gen 30:9-24

The rivalry was deep and lifelong, but both women could keep the peace and stay in their place without rancour.

So Jacob sent and called Rachel and Leah to the field, to his flock, and said to them," I see your father's countenance, that it is not favourable toward me as before; but the God of my father has been with me. And you know that with all my might I have served your father. Yet your father has deceived me and changed my wages ten times, but God did not allow him to hurt me. Gen 31:4-8

Then Rachel and Leah answered and said to him,"Is there still any portion or inheritance for us in our father's house? Are we not considered strangers by him? For he has sold us, and also completely consumed our money. For all these riches which God has taken from our father are really ours and our children's; now then, whatever God has said to you, do it." Then Jacob rose and set his sons and his wives on camel. Gen 31:14-18

At the time they left, Laban was some distance away, shearing his sheep. Rachel stole her father's household idols and took them with her. Gen 31:19-20

Laban caught up with Jacob as he was camped in the hill country of Gilead, and he set up his camp not far from Jacob's. "What do you mean by stealing away like this?" Laban demanded. "How dare you drag my daughters away like prisoners of war? Why did you slip away secretly? Why did you steal away? And why didn't you say you wanted to leave? I would have given you a farewell feast, with singing and music, accompanied by tambourines and harps. Why didn't you let me kiss my daughters and grandchildren and tell them good-bye? You have acted very foolishly! I could destroy you, but the God of your father appeared to me last night and warned me, 'Leave Jacob alone!' I can understand your feeling that you must go, and your intense longing for your father's home. But why have you stolen my gods?"

Then Laban replied to Jacob, "These women are my daughters, these children are my grandchildren, and these flocks are my flocks—in fact, everything you see is mine. But what can I do now about my daughters and their children? So come, let's make a covenant, you and I, and it will be a witness to our commitment." Gen 31:43-44 NLT

But it was also called Mizpah (which means "watchtower"), for Laban said, "May the Lord keep watch between us to make sure that we keep this covenant when we are out of each other's sight. If you mistreat my daughters or if you marry other wives, God will see it even if no one else does. He is a witness to this covenant between us. Gen 31:49-50 NLT

Rachel stole her father's idol. Why? Some theologians say it was because the person in possession of the household idols would be the person with rights to Laban's properties. Hence the reason Laban and Jacob had to make a covenant to never come after each other. Read Gen 31:51-54

So Jacob took an oath before the fearsome God of his father, Isaac, to respect the boundary line.

Jacob did not know Rachel stole her father's idol, and while trying to prove his innocence, he laid a curse on whoever the culprit was. See, *"I rushed away because I was afraid," Jacob answered. "I thought you would take your daughters from me by force. But as for your gods, see if you can find them, and let the person who has taken them die! And if you find anything else that belongs to you, identify it before all these relatives of ours, and I will give it back!" But Jacob did not know that Rachel had stolen the household idols. Laban went first into Jacob's tent to search there, then into Leah's, and then the tents of the two servant wives—but he found nothing. Finally, he went into Rachel's tent. But Rachel had taken the household idols and hidden them in her camel saddle, and now she was sitting on them. When Laban had thoroughly searched her tent without finding them, she said to her father, "Please, sir, forgive me if I don't get up for you. I'm having my monthly period."*

So Laban continued his search, but he could not find the household idols. Gen 31:25-35 NLT

Rachel, what a woman!

> *But Rachel went into labour while they were still some distance away. Her labour pains were intense. After a very hard delivery, the midwife finally exclaimed, "Don't be afraid—you have another son!" Rachel was about to die, but with her last breath she named the baby Ben-oni (which means "son of my sorrow"). The baby's father, however, called him Benjamin (which means "son of my right hand"). So Rachel died and was buried on the way to Ephrath (that is, Bethlehem). Jacob set up a stone monument over Rachel's grave, and it can be seen there to this day.* Gen 35:16-20

Some people believe she died because of the curse. Some think she died because she had hard labour. This brings us to some sensitive questions... if Rachel, the wife of Jacob (Israel) died from childbearing complications, is it right for people to refuse medical options that aid child delivery by saying they must give birth like the Hebrew women? Do they have statistics of mortality caused by hard labour? Would Rachel have refused to have a caesarean section if it could have saved her life? Would she have refused an epidural if she had a choice? Would her husband have thought she was less a woman for using available medical aids to birth their son? Is it a sin to accept help- using a midwife is already accepting help or what do you think?

Childbearing is the most vulnerable stage of a woman's life. Let her trust in God's grace instead of trying to prove her strength. God is gracious and kind, and all glory belongs to Him.

Bilhah and Zilpah

Bilhah and Zilpah were the maids of Rachel and Leah. They were put through what Sarah did to Hagar. They responded differently by not trying to usurp their mistresses and lived peacefully. But I don't know if they were happy; because the absence of war does not mean the presence of joy.

They were made surrogate mothers with no one seeking their opinion. In this time and day, no woman should be made to live like a maid\slave; without the power or right to decide what happens to her sex life or who she gets to be married to. Sadly, in some places, such things still happen through human trafficking and forced marriages. But we will not stop advocating for women's rights until the rights are given.

There was another twist in Bilhah's life. She slept with her stepson. She probably suffered from a lack of direction after being asked to have sex with her master at the wimps and caprices of her mistress. One repercussion of such sexual transactions is the emotional scars and baggage that cause a lapse of sound judgement.

Then Jacob travelled on and camped beyond Migdal-eder. While he was living there, Reuben had intercourse with Bilhah, his father's concubine, and Jacob soon heard about it. Gen 35:21-22

Sometimes, one sexual indiscretion leads to another.

Dinah

One day Dinah, the daughter of Jacob and Leah, went to visit some of the young women who lived in the area. But when the local prince, Shechem son of Hamor the Hivite, saw Dinah, he seized her and raped her. But then he fell in love with her, and he tried to win her affection with tender words. He said to his father, Hamor, "Get me this young girl. I want to marry her."

Soon Jacob heard that Shechem had defiled his daughter, Dinah. But since his sons were out in the fields herding his livestock, he said nothing until they returned. Hamor, Shechem's father, came to discuss the matter with Jacob. Meanwhile, Jacob's sons had come in from the field as soon as they heard what had happened. They were shocked and furious that their sister had been raped. Shechem had done a disgraceful thing against Jacob's family, something that should never be done.

Hamor tried to speak with Jacob and his sons. "My son Shechem is truly in love with your daughter," he said. "Please let him marry her. In fact, let's arrange other marriages, too. You give us your daughters for our sons, and we will give you our daughters for your sons. And you may live among us; the land is open to you! Settle here and trade with us. And feel free to buy property in the area."

Then Shechem himself spoke to Dinah's father and brothers. "Please be kind to me, and let me marry her," he begged. "I will give you whatever you ask. No matter what dowry or gift you demand, I will gladly pay it—just give me the girl as my wife." But since Shechem had defiled their sister, Dinah, Jacob's sons responded deceitfully to Shechem and his father, Hamor. They said to them, "We couldn't possibly allow this, because you're not circumcised. It would be a disgrace for our sister to marry a man like you! But here is a solution. If every man among you will be circumcised like we are, then we will give you our daughters, and we'll take your daughters for ourselves. We will live among you and become one people. But if you don't agree to be circumcised, we will take her and be on our way. Hamor and his son Shechem agreed to their proposal.

So all the men in the town council agreed with Hamor and Shechem, and every male in the town was circumcised. But three days later, when their wounds were still sore, two of Jacob's sons, Simeon and Levi, who were Dinah's full brothers, took their swords and entered the town without opposition. Then they slaughtered every male there, including Hamor and his son Shechem. They killed them with their swords, then took Dinah from Shechem's house and returned to their camp. Meanwhile, the rest of Jacob's sons arrived. Finding the men slaughtered, they plundered the town because their sister had been defiled there. Gen 1:-28NLT

An entire city was destroyed because of rape. Do not be deceived, rape is not a light or insignificant incident. Rape is the act of using duress to make someone have sex or be intimate with you. Rape is an unlawful sexual activity; forceful unwanted coitus, anal, oral or verbal intercourse. Rape is an incestuous action punishable by law. Rape is a sign of moral degradation, wickedness, lack of self-control and stupidity. Rape violates a person's right to avoid sex, be left alone or undefiled.

I wish Shechem bridled his desire and did things the right way... you don't come talking about love after raping someone. Rape is an action devoid of love and respect and it can ruin all chances of developing a healthy relationship.

Rape is so terrible, Jacobs's sons believed it was worth destroying a whole community over. And we know they were right because rape is an attack; a cruel violation that enrages sane people so much, the only thing that can attempt to soothe their hurt is justice. Dinah was a victim of rape like Tamar, but in her case, her rapist didn't deny culpability or blatantly reject her. Rather, he was willing to pay her family any price to atone. He wanted to marry her, but her brothers vehemently refused. They didn't think desiring to marry her could make up for what he did. As men, they probably know the depth of depravity any man who rapes a woman functions in, so they believed a rapist was unqualified to marry their sister. And thus, carried out justice on him by wiping out him and all the men in his village. That is how atrocious rape is!

Why didn't he just ask for her hand in marriage first? Why break in and steal? Why force her? Why should a man demean himself by raping a lady? Raping is a statement of inability, it's a confession of weakness.

If you like a lady and find her attractive, ask her nicely. If she says yes, and is willing to sleep with you, that's fine. If she says no, move on and try your luck elsewhere. If she says yes and later says no... move on and let her be. No woman deserves to be forced and no real man forces a woman, even if she walks around naked, because real men are not barbaric.

Violated

At this time before Israel had a king, there was a man of the tribe of Levi living on the far side of the hill country of Ephraim, who brought home a girl from Bethlehem in Judah to be his concubine. But she became angry with him and ran away, and returned to her father's home in Bethlehem, and was there about four months. Then her husband, taking along a servant and an extra donkey, went to see her to try to win her back again. When he arrived at her home, she let him in and introduced him to her father, who was delighted to meet him. Her father urged him to stay awhile, so he stayed three days, and they all had a very pleasant time.

On the fourth day they were up early, ready to leave, but the girl's father insisted on their having breakfast first. Then he pleaded with him to stay one more day, as they were having such a good time. At first the man refused, but his father-in-law kept urging him until finally he gave in. The next morning they were up early again, and again the girl's father pleaded, "Stay just today and leave sometime this evening." So they had another day of feasting.

That afternoon as he and his wife and servant were preparing to leave, his father-in-law said, "Look, it's getting late. Stay just tonight, and we will have a pleasant evening together and tomorrow you can get up early and be on your way."

But this time the man was adamant, so they left, getting as far as Jerusalem (also called Jebus) before dark.

His servant said to him, "It's getting too late to travel; let's stay here tonight."

"No," his master said, "we can't stay in this heathen city where there are no Israelites-we will go on to Gibeah, or possibly Ramah."

So they went on. The sun was setting just as they came to Gibeah, a village of the tribe of Benjamin, so they went there for the night. But as no one invited them in, they camped in the village square. Just then an old man came by on his way home from his work in the fields. (He was originally from the hill country of Ephraim, but was living now in Gibeah, even though it was in the territory of Benjamin.) When he saw the travellers camped in the square, he asked them where they were from and where they were going.

"We're on the way home from Bethlehem, in Judah," the man replied. "I live on the far edge of the Ephraim hill country, near Shiloh. But no one has taken us in for the night, even though we have fodder for our donkeys and plenty of food and wine for ourselves."

"Don't worry," the old man said, "be my guests; for you mustn't stay here in the square. It's too dangerous."

So he took them home with him. He fed their donkeys while they rested, and afterward they had supper together. Just as they were beginning to warm to the occasion, a gang of sex perverts gathered around the house and began beating at the door and yelling at the old man to bring out the man who was staying with him, so they could rape him. The old man stepped outside to talk to them.

"No, my brothers, don't do such a dastardly act," he begged, "for he is my guest. Here, take my virgin daughter and this man's wife. I'll bring them out and you can do whatever you like to them-but don't do such a thing to this man."

But they wouldn't listen to him. <u>Then the girl's husband pushed her out to them,</u> and they abused her all night, taking turns raping her until morning. Finally, just at dawn, they let her go. She fell down at the door of the house and lay there until it was light. When her husband opened the door to be on his way, he found her there, fallen down in front of the door with her hands digging into the threshold.

"Well, come on," he said. "Let's get going."

But there was no answer, for she was dead; so he threw her across the donkey's back and took her home. When he got there he took a knife and cut her body into twelve parts and sent one piece to each tribe of Israel. Then the entire nation was roused to action against the men of Benjamin because of this awful deed.

"There hasn't been such a horrible crime since Israel left Egypt," everyone said. "We've got to do something about it." Judg 19:1-30TLB

All the people were at once and as one person on their feet. "None of us will go home; not a single one of us will go to his own house. Here's our plan for dealing with Gibeah: We'll march against it by drawing lots. Judg 20:8-10 MESSAGE

Rape is an outrageous act. One thing that caught my attention as I read the above passage was the fact that her husband pushed her out to save himself. Several times, people enable rape by being selfish and uncaring. It reminded me of the story of a young girl who was consistently being raped by her stepfather. Her mother knew of it but pretended because she didn't want to lose her marriage. Whenever the young girl tried to talk with her, she would accuse her of lying and shush her up. Why did the person who was supposed to protect her offer her? Because she thought it was just sex, it was a small price to pay?

The truth is, forceful sex is never a small price to pay! There is nothing casual or harmless about it, it is a violation that even justice can never fully repair.

Tamar

After this Absalom the son of David had a lovely sister, whose name was Tamar; and Amnon the son of David loved her. Amnon was so distressed over his sister Tamar that he became sick; for she was a virgin. And it was improper for Amnon to do anything to her. But Amnon had a friend whose name was Jonadab the son of Shimeah, David's brother. Now Jonadab was a very crafty man. And he said to him, "Why are you, the king's son, becoming thinner day after day? Will you not tell me?"

Amnon said to him, "I love Tamar, my brother Absalom's sister." So Jonadab said to him, "Lie down on your bed and pretend to be ill. And when your father comes to see you, say to him, 'Please let my sister Tamar come and give me food, and prepare the food in my sight, that I may see it and eat it from her hand.'" Then Amnon lay down and pretended to be ill; and when the king came to see him, Amnon said to the king, "Please let Tamar my sister come and make a couple of cakes for me in my sight, that I may eat from her hand." And David sent home to Tamar, saying, "Now go to your brother Amnon's house, and prepare food for him." So Tamar went to her brother Amnon's house; and he was lying down. Then she took flour and kneaded it, made cakes in his sight, and baked the cakes. 9 And she took the pan and placed them out before him, but he refused to eat. Then Amnon said, "Have everyone go out from me." And they all went out from him. Then Amnon said to Tamar, "Bring the food into the bedroom, that I may eat from your hand." And Tamar took the cakes which she had made, and brought them to Amnon her brother in the bedroom.

Now when she had brought them to him to eat, he took hold of her and said to her, "Come, lie with me, my sister." But she answered him, "No, my brother, do not force me, for no such thing should be done in Israel. Do not do this disgraceful thing! And I, where could I take my shame? And as for you, you would be like one of the fools in Israel. Now therefore, please speak to the king; for he will not withhold me from you."

In the above scripture, Tamar pleaded with her rapist; she tried to talk sense into him but as the fool that she was telling him not to be, he ignored her. See, *"However, he would not heed her voice; and being stronger than she, he forced her and lay with her. Then Amnon hated her exceedingly, so that the hatred with which he hated her was greater than the love with which he had loved her. And Amnon said to her, "Arise, be gone!"* 2 Sam 13:1-15

"No, no!" she cried. "To reject me now is a greater crime than the other you did to me."

But he wouldn't listen to her. He shouted for his valet and demanded, "Throw this woman out and lock the door behind her." So he put her out. She was wearing a long robe with sleeves, as was the custom in those days for virgin daughters of the king. Now she tore the robe and put ashes on her head and with her head in her hands went away crying. Her brother Absalom asked her, "Is it true that Amnon raped you? Don't be so upset, since it's all in the family anyway. It's not anything to worry about!" So Tamar lived as a desolate woman in her brother Absalom's quarters.

When King David heard what had happened, he was very angry, but Absalom said nothing one way or the other about this to Amnon. However, he hated him with a deep hatred because of what he had done to his sister. 2 Sam 13:16-22 TLB

Absalom prepared a banquet fit for a king. Then he instructed his servants, "Look sharp, now. When Amnon is well into the sauce and feeling no pain, and I give the order 'Strike Amnon,' kill him. And don't be afraid — I'm the one giving the command. Courage! You can do it!" 2 Sam 13:28

Absalom killed Amnon, his stepbrother, for raping and rejecting Tamar, his sister. Tamar, the daughter of David, was a young lady betrayed by Amnon; someone who, as a stepbrother, owed her a duty of protection in reward for her trust.

Rape is an attack and invasion. It never leaves the victims the way they were. The experience is deeply horrifying and it will take some victims forever to get over it if they ever do.

To any Tamar out there; violated, cheated on and robbed of the one thing that should be yours to give or to keep. May God comfort you. I pray for healing, restoration, justice and peace.

Tamar said that the rejection was worse than the rape. The lies, the denial, the stigma, and the lack of responsibility were heart-breaking. Rape victims deserve acknowledgement, apology, justice and love to help them find closure.

Raping a woman is equal to imprisoning her and forcing her to live a life of desolation. It is a wicked thing and only done by insecure, uninformed, unwise men with a lack of self-control and moral decency.

Everyone should be transparent and just in exercising the gift of trust given to them. Being male does not rob anyone of the ability to exercise self-control and be decent. As a man, you can find anybody attractive, but remember it is their body, and it is their right. A gentleman will let anyone he wants to get sexual with the choice. And stay away from under-aged people who don't know enough to decide for themselves.

Some ladies, like Tamar, were raped by a familiar person. A shameless, irresponsible person who abused the gift of trust. Rape is never the fault of the victims, rather; it is a testament to the selfishness and perversity of the rapist. I remember the story of a young girl who was sexually abused by her uncle. Why did he damage her purity? Rape is one of the highest expressions of selfishness. That was why her uncle couldn't care that his action was hurting her body or damaging her person. He couldn't care that he was corrupting her mind and robbing her of the ability to exercise self-control over her sexual urges. Lack of self-control is one damage sexual abuse and exploitation can cause. (An unrepentant rapist is a person who is a monster or who became a monster because they themselves were once victims).

Thus, a more pressing question is, why should anyone want to act like it never happened? Knowing it could even result in a chain reaction because lack of accountability makes the cycle continue. Why should anyone protect the culprit and deny the victim justice? . . . The lies and cover-ups embolden the rapist. The lack of interest is worse because it means the world is saying that it doesn't matter whether the victim was raped. It is a passive way of normalizing a vice. This is partly the reason there seemed to be an increase in the number of paedophiles. When sexually abused children see their abusers, who may be close family members, carrying on with their lives like they did nothing wrong, they may not find moral justification to not replicate their actions. They may feel that nobody is going to hold them accountable as well.

Denying rape victims justice and blaming them does not only result in the deadening of conscience. It also messes with the psychology of the victim by causing lingering fear and confusion. Which makes it harder for them to find closure and move on.

As a society, we need to stop victimising the victim, blaming the innocent and being an accomplice to evil. Before you judge a rape victim and unsympathetically ask, "what was she doing there? Or why was she there alone?" Answer this question: Have you ever visited a male before, any male? Have you been alone with a member of the opposite sex, even your father? If you have, you are not more careful or less deserving of rape than the victims you dare condemn.

Dear Tamar, it was not your fault. When you visited that friend/ uncle/ teacher who turned out to be a rapist, you probably thought you were dealing with a normal person. You didn't know you were dealing with an unregenerate. It was not your fault.

I am thankful for the increasing number of interest groups and NGOs working tirelessly to create awareness, get justice and provide support to rape victims. Dear Tamar, dear Dinah please try to carry on, don't stop living your life. We are praying for you. God comfort, strengthen and bless you.

Gomer; Hosea's wife

When the Lord began to speak through Hosea, the Lord said to him, "Go, take to yourself an adulterous wife and children of unfaithfulness, because the land is guilty of the vilest adultery in departing from the Lord." So he married Gomer daughter of Diblaim, and she conceived and bore him a son. Then the Lord said to Hosea, "Call him Jezreel, because I will soon punish the house of Jehu for the massacre at Jezreel, and I will put an end to the kingdom of Israel. In that day I will break Israel's bow in the Valley of Jezreel." Gomer conceived again and gave birth to a daughter. Then the Lord said to Hosea, "Call her Lo-Ruhamah, for I will no longer show love to the house of Israel, that I should at all forgive them. Yet I will show love to the house of Judah; and I will save them — not by bow, sword or battle, or by horses and horsemen, but by the Lord their God." After she had weaned Lo-Ruhamah, Gomer had another son. Then the Lord said, "Call him Lo-Ammi, for you are not my people, and I am not your God. Hos 1:2-9 NIV*

God asked Hosea to marry Gomer, a known prostitute, to emblematize the unfaithfulness of Israel to GOD. Israel had turned away from God's ways and was living in sin. From biblical narratives, idol worship is synonymous with prostituting.

From the story of Gomer, we see how much God hates unrighteousness; we learn he judges unfaithfulness; we know that His love is unfailing.

Say of your brothers, 'My people,' and of your sisters, 'My loved one.'

"Rebuke your mother, rebuke her, for she is not my wife, and I am not her husband. Let her remove the adulterous look from her face and the unfaithfulness from between her breasts. Otherwise I will strip her naked and make her as bare as on the day she was born; I will make her like a desert, turn her into a parched land, and slay her with thirst. I will not show my love to her children, because they are the children of adultery. Their mother has been unfaithful and has conceived them in disgrace. <u>*She said, 'I will go after my lovers, who give me my food and my water, my wool and my linen, my oil and my drink.'*</u> Hos 2:1-5 NIV

Therefore I will block her path with thornbushes; I will wall her in so that she cannot find her way. She will chase after her lovers but not catch them; she will look for them but not find them. Then she will say, 'I will go back to my husband as at first, for then I was better off than now.'
<u>*She has not acknowledged that I was the one who gave her the grain, the new wine and oil,*</u> *who lavished on her the silver and gold — which they used for Baal. "Therefore I will take away my grain when it ripens, and my new wine when it is ready. I will take back my wool and my linen, intended to cover her nakedness.* Hos 2:6-9 NIV

Her life also epitomises the connection between wantonness and delusions of lack. She thought she was being sustained by her numerous affairs. Just the same way some people think they are successful because of their lack of scruples, sheer determination and refusal to acknowledge God.

Her story demystifies the struggle of a spouse who has a cheating and undependable partner.

> *"Therefore I am now going to allure her; I will lead her into the desert and speak tenderly to her. There I will give her back her vineyards, and will make the Valley of Achor a door of hope.*
> *There she will sing as in the days of her youth, as in the day she came up out of Egypt. "In that day," declares the Lord, "you will call me 'my husband'; you will no longer call me 'my master.' I will remove the names of the Baals from her lips; no longer will their names be invoked. In that day I will make a covenant for them with the beasts of the field and the birds of the air and the creatures that move along the ground.* Hos 2:14-18 NIV

Gomer symbolises the disloyalty of man to God. Despite man's callousness, fickleness and ignorance, God remains faithful to the relationship. God wants the sinner to repent and return to him. He will love you anew. He comes after you with yet another mind-blowing offer - JESUS CHRIST.

The Strange Women

The bible warns us several times about 'the strange woman'. But who is the strange woman?

The strange woman is referred to as an immoral woman, a forbidden woman, an adulteress, a harlot, a seductress and an idolator.

> *Wisdom will save you from the ways of wicked men, from men whose words are perverse, who leave the straight paths to walk in dark ways, who delight in doing wrong and rejoice in the perverseness of evil, whose paths are crooked and who are devious in their ways.*
>
> *It will save you also from the adulteress from the wayward wife with her seductive words, who has left the partner of her youth and ignored the covenant she made before God. For her house leads down to death and her paths to the spirits of the dead. None who go to her return or attain the paths of life.* Prov 2:12-19 NIV

> *"For the lips of a strange woman drop as an honeycomb, and her mouth is smoother than oil: But her end is bitter as wormwood, sharp as a two edged sword.* Prov 5:3

> *The lips of a <u>seductive woman</u> are oh so sweet, her soft words are oh so smooth. But it won't be long before she's gravel in your mouth, a pain in your gut, a wound in your heart.* MESSAGE

For the commandment is a lamp, and the law a light; Reproofs of instruction are the way of life, To keep you from the evil woman ,from the flattering tongue of a seductress. Do not lust after her beauty in your heart, Nor let her allure you with her eyelids. For by means of a harlot a man is reduced to a crust of bread and an adulteress will prey upon his precious life. Prov 6:23-26

My son, keep my words, and lay up my commandments with thee. Keep my commandments, and live; and my law as the apple of thine eye. Bind them upon thy fingers, write them upon the table of thine heart. Say unto wisdom, Thou art my sister; and call understanding thy kinswoman: That they may keep thee from the <u>*strange woman*</u>*, from the* <u>*stranger*</u> *which flattereth with her words.* Prov 7:1-5 KJV

A prostitute is a dangerous trap; a promiscuous woman is as dangerous as falling into a narrow well. She hides and waits like a robber, eager to make more men unfaithful. Prov 23:27-28

Let them protect you from an affair with <u>an immoral woman</u>*, from listening to the* <u>flattery of a promiscuous woman</u>*. While I was at the window of my house, looking through the curtain, I saw some naive young men, and one in particular who lacked common sense. He was crossing the street near the house of an immoral woman, strolling down the path by her house.* Prov 7:4-8 NLT

My son, pay attention to my wisdom; listen carefully to my wise counsel. Then you will show discernment, and your lips will express what you've learned. For the lips of an <u>*immoral woman*</u> *are as sweet as honey, and her mouth is smoother than oil. But in the end she is as bitter as poison, as dangerous as a double-edged sword. Her feet go down to death; her steps lead straight to the grave. For she cares nothing about the path to life. She staggers down a crooked trail and doesn't realize it. So now, my sons, listen to me. Never stray from what I am about to say:* PROV 5:1-7NLT

Keep your distance from such a woman; absolutely stay out of her neighbourhood. You don't want to squander your wonderful life, to waste your precious life among the hard-hearted. Why should you allow strangers to take advantage of you?

Why be exploited by those who care nothing for you? You don't want to end your life full of regrets, nothing but sin and bones, Saying, "Oh, why didn't I do what they told me? Why did I reject a disciplined life? Why didn't I listen to my mentors, or take my teachers seriously? Prov 5:8-13 MESSAGE

I took part in almost every kind of evil, and the whole community knew it." Drink the water from your own cistern, fresh water from your own well. Let what your springs produce be dispersed outside, streams of water flowing in the streets; but let them be for you alone and not for strangers with you. Let your fountain, the wife of your youth, be blessed; find joy in her — a lovely deer, a graceful fawn; let her breasts satisfy you at all times, always be infatuated with her love.

My son, why be infatuated with an unknown woman? Why embrace the body of a loose woman? For Adonai is watching a man's ways; he surveys all his paths. A wicked person's own crimes will trap him, he will be held fast by the ropes of his sin.

He will die from lack of discipline; the magnitude of his folly will make him totter and fall. Prov 5:14-23 CJB

What else can I say? A word is enough for the wise. Being male is not a license to have indiscriminate sex.

Adultery

Adonai said to Moshe, "Tell the people of Isra'el, 'If a man's wife goes astray and is unfaithful to him; that is, if another man goes to bed with her without her husband's knowledge, so that she becomes impure secretly, and there is no witness against her, and she was not caught in the act; then, if a spirit of jealousy comes over him, and he is jealous of his wife, and she has become impure — or, for that matter, if the spirit of jealousy comes over him, and he is jealous of his wife, and she has not become impure — he is to bring his wife to the cohen, along with the offering for her, two quarts of barley flour on which he has not poured olive oil or put frankincense, because it is a grain offering for jealousy, a grain offering for remembering, for recalling guilt to mind. The cohen will bring her forward and place her before Adonai. The cohen will put holy water in a clay pot, and then the cohen will take some of the dust on the floor of the tabernacle and put it in the water. The cohen will place the woman before Adonai, unbind the woman's hair and put the grain offering for remembering in her hands, the grain offering for jealousy; while the cohen has in his hand the water of embitterment and cursing. The cohen will make her swear by saying to her, "If no man has gone to bed with you, if you have not gone astray to make yourself unclean while under your husband's authority, then be free from this water of embitterment and cursing. But if you have in fact gone astray while under your husband's authority and become unclean, because some man other than your husband has gone to bed with you . . ." then the cohen is to make the woman swear with an oath that includes a curse; the cohen will say to the woman, ". . .may Adonai make you an object of cursing and condemnation among your people by making your private parts shrivel and your abdomen swell up! May this water that causes the curse go into your inner parts and make your abdomen swell and your private parts shrivel up!" — and the woman is to respond, "Amen! Amen!" The cohen is to write these curses on a scroll, wash them off into the water of embitterment and make the woman drink the water of embitterment and cursing — the water of cursing will enter her and become bitter. Then the cohen is to remove the grain offering for jealousy from the woman's hand, wave the grain offering before Adonai and bring it to the altar. The cohen is to take a handful of the grain offering as its reminder portion and make it go up in smoke on the altar; afterwards, he is to make the woman drink the water. When he has made her drink the water, then, if she is unclean and has been unfaithful to her husband, the water that causes the curse will enter her and become bitter, so that her abdomen swells and her private parts shrivel up; and the woman will become an object of cursing among her people. But if the woman is not unclean but clean, then she will be innocent and will have children. This is the law for jealousy: when either a wife under her husband's authority goes astray and becomes unclean, or the spirit of jealousy comes over a husband and he becomes jealous of his wife, then he is to place the woman before Adonai, and the cohen is to deal with her in accordance with all of this law. The husband will be clear of guilt, but the wife will bear the consequences of her guilt." Num 5:11-31 CJB

Oholah and Oholibah

"And because you have forgotten me and turned your back on me, this is what the Sovereign Lord says: You must bear the consequences of all your lewdness and prostitution."

The LORD's Judgment on Both Sisters

The Lord said to me, "Son of man, you must accuse Oholah and Oholibah of all their detestable sins. They have committed both adultery and murder—adultery by worshiping idols and murder by burning as sacrifices the children they bore to me. Furthermore, they have defiled my Temple and violated my Sabbath day! On the very day that they sacrificed their children to their idols, they boldly came into my Temple to worship! They came in and defiled my house.

"You sisters sent messengers to distant lands to get men. Then when they arrived, you bathed yourselves, painted your eyelids, and put on your finest jewels for them. You sat with them on a beautifully embroidered couch and put my incense and my special oil on a table that was spread before you. From your room came the sound of many men carousing. They were lustful men and drunkards from the wilderness, who put bracelets on your wrists and beautiful crowns on your heads. Then I said, 'If they really want to have sex with old worn-out prostitutes like these, let them!' And that is what they did. They had sex with

Oholah and Oholibah, these shameless prostitutes. But righteous people will judge these sister cities for what they really are— adulterers and murderers.

*"Now this is what the Sovereign Lord says: Bring an army against them and hand them over to be terrorized and plundered. For their enemies will stone them and kill them with swords. They will butcher their sons and daughters and burn their homes. In this way, I will put an end to lewdness and idolatry in the land, and my judgment will be a warning to others not to follow their wicked example. You will be fully repaid for all your prostitution—your worship of idols. Yes, you will suffer the full penalty. Then you will know that I am the Sovereign Lord."*Ezek 23:35-49 NLT

Potiphar's Wife

And it came to pass after these things that his master's wife cast longing eyes on Joseph, and she said, "Lie with me." But he refused and said to his master's wife, "Look, my master does not know what is with me in the house, and he has committed all that he has to my hand. There is no one greater in this house than I, nor has he kept back anything from me but you, because you are his wife. How then can I do this great wickedness, and sin against God?" So it was, as she spoke to Joseph day by day, that he did not heed her, to lie with her or to be with her. But it happened about this time, when Joseph went into the house to do his work, and none of the men of the house was inside, that she caught him by his garment, saying, "Lie with me." But he left his garment in her hand, and fled and ran outside. And so it was, when she saw that he had left his garment in her hand and fled outside, that she called to the men of her house and spoke to them, saying, "See, he has brought in to us a Hebrew to mock us. He came in to me to lie with me, and I cried out with a loud voice. And it happened, when he heard that I lifted my voice and cried out, that he left his garment with me, and fled and went outside." So she kept his garment with her until his master came home. Then she spoke to him with words like these, saying, "The Hebrew servant whom you brought to us came in to me to mock me; so it happened, as I lifted my voice and cried out, that he left his garment with me and fled outside." So it was, when his master heard the words which his wife spoke to him, saying, "Your servant did to me after this manner," that his anger was aroused. Then Joseph's master took him and put him into the prison, a place where the king's prisoners were confined. And he was there in the prison.

Before the real glory, you will be tested with camouflage glory. Sometimes we mistake this counterfeit miracle for the break we have been waiting for. Joseph was a young man who had suffered rejection, betrayal, loss and other hardships, having gone through so much suffering, he could have viewed Potiphar's wife's interest as divine intervention. He could have decided to sin and repent later but he didn't. When people fall for the camouflage, they might never know what they have missed. They feel pleased with the success they got through compromise because they don't know they have just traded durable success for sin induced promotion.

Potiphar's wife was a distraction in Joseph's path. Thankfully, Joseph was grounded and moral, otherwise, his dream of being a leader may never have been actualised. Chances are his boss would have found out about the affair and he may have lost his life. Having an affair with Potiphar's wife would have been sinning against God, and without God on his side, he may never have made it. The trickiest part of this is that anybody can play the role of Potiphar's wife. Will you know when camouflage glory tempts you?

Joseph knew that adultery was a sin and so would not be enticed by any pleasure or advantage sleeping with her was going to give him. The only way to differentiate between a counterfeit promotion and a real one is that the counterfeit will demand you tread your values on the ground. Like joseph, avoid anything that is against God's Word.

Congreve said hell has no fury like a woman scorned. Potiphar's wife proved how furious a woman gets when her advances are shunned. She got Joseph, an innocent man, put behind bars. I wonder how she slept each night knowing he was languishing in prison for honouring God and respecting her husband. The way Joseph's life turned out is an encouragement to us because it shows us that God will vindicate and give double honour for the shame the enemy tried to hang on us.

When God is ready to lift you, He does not consult with your detractors. He shocks them into silence and renders them irrelevant. We never had of Potiphar's wife again. Who knows what became of her?

Samson's First Woman

Samson's first woman…Her only offence was that a powerful man loved her. I felt sorry for this young bride, who was forced to betray her husband, not for money but to protect her family.

Samson went down to Timnah and saw there a young Philistine woman. When he returned, he said to his father and mother, "I have seen a Philistine woman in Timnah; now get her for me as my wife." His father and mother replied, "Isn't there an acceptable woman among your relatives or among all our people? Must you go to the uncircumcised Philistines to get a wife?" But Samson said to his father, "Get her for me. She's the right one for me." (His parents did not know that this was from the LORD, who was seeking an occasion to confront the Philistines; for at that time they were ruling over Israel.) Samson went down to Timnah together with his father and mother. As they approached the vineyards of Timnah, suddenly a young lion came roaring toward him. The Spirit of the LORD came upon him in power so that he tore the lion apart with his bare hands as he might have torn a young goat. But he told neither his father nor his mother what he had done. Then he went down and talked with the woman, and he liked her.

Some time later, when he went back to marry her, he turned aside to look at the lion's carcass. In it was a swarm of bees and some honey, which he scooped out with his hands and ate as he went along. When he rejoined his parents, he gave them some, and they too ate it. But he did not tell them that he had taken the honey from the lion's carcass. Now his father went down to see the woman. And Samson made a feast there, as was customary for bridegrooms. When he appeared, he was given thirty companions. Judg 14:1-11 NIV

Then Samson said to them, "Let me pose a riddle to you. If you can correctly solve and explain it to me within the seven days of the feast, then I will give you thirty linen garments and thirty changes of clothing. But if you cannot explain it to me, then you shall give me thirty linen garments and thirty changes of clothing."And they said to him,"Pose your riddle, that we may hear it." So he said to them:"Out of the eater came something to eat, And out of the strong came something sweet." Now for three days they could not explain the riddle.

But it came to pass on the seventh day that they said to Samson's wife,"Entice your husband, that he may explain the riddle to us, or else we will burn you and your father's house with fire. Have you invited us in order to take what is ours? Is that not so?"

Then Samson's wife wept on him, and said,"You only hate me! You do not love me! You have posed a riddle to the sons of my people, but you have not explained it to me."

And he said to her, "Look, I have not explained it to my father or my mother; so should I explain it to you?" Now she had wept on him the seven days while their feast lasted. And it happened on the seventh day that he told her, because she pressed him so

much. Then she explained the riddle to the sons of her people. So the men of the city said to him on the seventh day before the sun went down:

"What is sweeter than honey?

And what is stronger than a lion?"

And he said to them:"If you had not plowed with my heifer, You would not have solved my riddle!" Judg 14:12-18

All she probably wanted was to marry and be happy. When she said "yes", she never bargained on endangering herself and her relatives. Sometimes, life presents twists and turns. We do not have the full picture all the time, and things may seem beyond our control. At such times, all we can do is pray for wisdom so that we will never be victims of the depravity and wickedness of men.

One key lesson here is the **danger of lack of communication**. I think she should have told Samson about the threat, but it seems she didn't know him well enough to trust him to protect her and her family. Sometimes we underestimate those close to us; we seem to have more faith in the enemy's ability to hurt us than in the friend's ability to protect us. How I wish she had more faith in her husband.

Lesson two: Influence of women.

That the women Samson loved were approached by his enemies and propositioned to expose his secrets also points to the indisputable **influence of women.** A woman can make or mar a man in a way and speed that his fellow man cannot; truly a man is only as great as the woman he is with. For a man to sustain his greatness and strength, he needs to cultivate strength of character, loyalty and wisdom into his woman, even if they were not there before. Failure to do that may be disastrous because every great man has enemies and enemies fight with tools they think are effective. History is replete with tales of women who have been used as effective weapons. Motivated by greed, fear or naivete, these women were injurious to their partners.

> *And the Spirit of the Lord rushed upon him, and he went down to Ashkelon and struck down thirty men of the town and took their spoil and gave the garments to those who had told the riddle. In hot anger he went back to his father's house. And Samson's wife was given to his companion, who had been his best man. . .*

Lesson 3: Knowledge versus Assumption.

Seek to know instead of finding comfort in assumptions. Samson's wife probably did not tell him about the threat because she felt she could handle it. She might have thought Samson's hurt and wrath were nothing compared to that of her countrymen. Whenever we assume how others may respond to a situation and decide based on those assumptions, we can make this error. She thought that once she did the deed, everything would be okay and Samson would understand. But it turned out that Samson was so wroth, he walked out of the marriage. And again, she and her family assumed he was permanently done.

After some days, at the time of wheat harvest, <u>Samson went to visit his wife with a young goat. And he said, "I will go in to my wife in the chamber." But her father would not allow him to go in. And her father said, "I really thought that you utterly hated her, so I gave her to your companion. Is not her younger sister more beautiful than she? Please take her instead." And Samson said to them,</u> "This time I shall be innocent in regard to the Philistines, when I do them harm." So Samson went and caught 300 foxes and took torches. And he turned them tail to tail and put a torch between each pair of tails. And when he had set fire to the torches, he let the foxes go into the standing grain of the Philistines and set fire to the stacked grain and the standing grain, as well as the olive orchards. Then the Philistines said, "Who has done this?" And they said, "Samson, the son-in-law of the Timnite, because he has taken his wife and given her to his companion." <u>And the Philistines came up and burned her and her father with fire.</u> And Samson said to them, "If this is what you do, I swear I will be avenged on you, and after that I will quit." And he struck them hip and thigh with a great blow, and he went down and stayed in the cleft of the rock of Etam. Judg 14:19-15:8 ESV

After watching the movie, 'the other Boleyn girl', my hatred for schemings, manipulations and deceit doubled. The very thing Samson's wife was trying to avoid still befell her and her family because she was dealing with unscrupulous people. Making a deal with unreasonable people never helps. They already hated her for bringing such a powerful man like Samson as her groom because Samson's people and their people are not particularly friends. So, they just needed an excuse to show how unregenerate they were.

I wish Samson exercised self-control; I wish he thought about his wife before doing the things he did. First, he walked away like the marriage was over and then he returned like he didn't walk away. And on seeing that his wife had been married off to someone else, he went on a destruction spree which led to his wife being killed. He avenged her death, but it was too late. Sometimes we hurt the ones we love the most, sometimes we leave the ones that need us behind, sometimes we learn only when the deed is done. Familiarity should not make us trivialise kindness, support and loyalty. Samson's wife hurt him because she felt he would understand. Samson went back to his country without taking his wife because he felt she would understand that he was just angry and would be back bearing gifts. He didn't realise she needed him; he didn't consider what her fate would be when he left her alone with angry, unscrupulous people. Quite sad, I cried while writing this chapter because many people are still making such errors today. Please, let's learn to be considerate, truthful and patient.

Delilah

Some time later Samson fell in love with a woman named Delilah, who lived in the valley of Sorek. The rulers of the Philistines went to her and said, "Entice Samson to tell you what makes him so strong and how he can be overpowered and tied up securely. Then each of us will give you 1,100 pieces of silver." So Delilah said to Samson, "Please tell me what makes you so strong and what it would take to tie you up securely." Samson replied, "If I were tied up with seven new bowstrings that have not yet been dried, I would become as weak as anyone else."

So, the Philistine rulers brought Delilah seven new bowstrings, and she tied Samson up with them. She had hidden some men in one of the inner rooms of her house, and she cried out, "Samson! The Philistines have come to capture you!" But Samson snapped the bowstrings as a piece of string snaps when it is burned by a fire. So the secret of his strength was not discovered. Afterward Delilah said to him, "You've been making fun of me and telling me lies! Now please tell me how you can be tied up securely." Samson replied, "If I were tied up with brand-new ropes that had never been used, I would become as weak as anyone else.

So, Delilah took new ropes and tied him up with them. The men were hiding in the inner room as before, and again Delilah cried out, "Samson! The Philistines have come to capture you!" But again Samson snapped the ropes from his arms as if they were thread Then

Delilah said, "You've been making fun of me and telling me lies! Now tell me how you can be tied up securely."

Samson replied, "If you were to weave the seven braids of my hair into the fabric on your loom and tighten it with the loom shuttle, I would become as weak as anyone else." So while he slept, Delilah wove the seven braids of his hair into the fabric. Then she tightened it with the loom shuttle. Again she cried out, "Samson! The Philistines have come to capture you!" But Samson woke up, pulled back the loom shuttle, and yanked his hair away from the loom and the fabric. Then Delilah pouted, "How can you tell me, 'I love you,' when you don't share your secrets with me? You've made fun of me three times now, and you still haven't told me what makes you so strong!" She tormented him with her nagging day after day until he was sick to death of it. Finally, Samson shared his secret with her. "My hair has never been cut," he confessed, "for I was dedicated to God as a Nazirite from birth. If my head were shaved, my strength would leave me, and I would become as weak as anyone else."

Delilah realized he had finally told her the truth, so she sent for the Philistine rulers. "Come back one more time," she said, "for he has finally told me his secret." So the Philistine rulers returned with the money in their hands. Delilah lulled Samson to sleep with his head in her lap, and then she called in a man to shave off the seven locks of his hair. In this way she began to bring him down and his strength left him. Then she cried out, "Samson! The Philistines have come to capture you!"

When he woke up, he thought, "I will do as before and shake myself free." But he didn't realize the Lord had left him. So the Philistines captured him and gouged out his eyes. They took him to

Gaza, where he was bound with bronze chains and forced to grind grain in the prison. Judg 16:4-21 NLT

Have you ever met someone who makes you feel bad about being cautious? Have you ever met people that wanted you to be vulnerable and yet used the information you gave them to hurt you? I have, and it was a traumatic experience. Such people are always quick to say, "trust me, I am a nice person".

Never trust a person just because they asked you to. Trust people because you think they are trustworthy. Relying on the Holy Spirit can guarantee a foolproof instinct and intuition you can trust.

Meeting a Delilah is the worst thing that can happen to the destiny of any man. The lords of the Philistines came to Delilah to help them find out the secret of the strength of Samson because she had access to Samson. They knew that if anyone could find and expose his vulnerability; it was only someone like the woman he loves. It is a terrible mistake to love the wrong person; it is calamitous to be with the wrong people.

Delilah asked Samson consistently and berated him for not telling her the source of his strength. She wore him with much nagging; she used emotional blackmail, doubted his love, challenged him to prove his love all because she had been bribed.

The fact that Samson would have been super careful about telling Delilah his secret because of what happened with his first love just tells us how persistent Delilah must have been to have eventually torn down his defences. As I studied this passage, I wondered why Samson did not walk away from such harassment.

And then the answer came. He didn't leave because he didn't know how dangerous disloyalty was. Samson underestimated the desperate wickedness and greed that could be resident in a fake lover's heart. He also probably thought, "I couldn't possibly be fooled twice". He forgot that a strategy that works hardly suffers from over-usage. Thus, he misjudged the situation by assuming Delilah was pestering him just out of natural and safe curiosity. He probably reacted the way you would react if someone you were dating asked you how rich your dad is. Or tell you to share a family secret. You will probably laugh it off and think it's not serious. You may not see it as a warning sign.

> *Judges 16:20 (KJV) "And she said, The Philistines be upon thee, Samson. And he awoke out of his sleep, and said, I will go out as at other times before, and shake myself. And he wist not that the Lord was departed from him."*

Delilah had the gift of access. He slept on her thighs. He could be vulnerable to her, and what did she do? She sold him out.

Everyone requires a place to unwind and a friend to trust. When they choose you, please do not be like Delilah; do not make trusting you a mistake. There is no grace there, never be the woman who gives other women a bad name; that makes men say all women are faithless, trash or unworthy of love and trust. Never be the person who makes others a fool for love; your personal decision to be true and kind will make the world a better place. Some women/ men think cheating others is a wise thing to do, but they are wrong. I beseech everyone in the name of God to hold fast to goodness, kindness and love. The rewards are boundless and eternal. A wise woman never makes trusting her a mistake.

Delilah abused her power. She had access to a man who everyone honoured, feared and loved. She was in a place of privilege, but she proved she didn't deserve it. And because Samson was vulnerable to the wrong person, it cost him his eyes, his assignments, his vision and his mission. The course of his life was altered because of this strange woman.

Commit your relationship to God and pray so you can see the warning signs. Lust makes anyone act strangely. That's the reason after Delilah asked Samson to tell her the source of his strength four times, he still didn't figure out something was wrong. With unbridled passion comes weakness... so, stay superior to lust by yielding yourselves to God. When asking God to lead and direct you, do not forget to ask for his opinion on your relationships too. God has something to say about who you hang around with, read the book of Proverbs and be wiser.

Jezebel

Jezebel was the wife of Ahab, she was the definition of evil and sexual wantonness. Almost everyone has heard about Jezebel at one point or another because Jezebel is always used as the perfect example whenever we want to talk about a decadent woman.

Today we will find out why. Let's read

> *In the thirty-eighth year of Asa king of Judah, Ahab son of Omri became king of Israel, and he reigned in Samaria over Israel twenty-two years. Ahab son of Omri did more evil in the eyes of the Lord than any of those before him. He not only considered it trivial to commit the sins of Jeroboam son of Nebat, but he also married Jezebel daughter of Ethbaal king of the Sidonians, and began to serve Baal and worship him.* 1 Kings 16:29-32NIV

> *But there was no one like Ahab who sold himself to do wickedness in the sight of the Lord, because Jezebel his wife stirred him up.* 1 Kings 21:25-26

1. Jezebel incited her husband to do evil.

The bible says none did evil like Ahab; and Ahab did such evil because his wife, Jezebel, stirred and incited him.

So Ahab went home, sullen and angry because Naboth the Jezreelite had said, "I will not give you the inheritance of my fathers." He lay on his bed sulking and refused to eat.

His wife Jezebel came in and asked him, "Why are you so sullen? Why won't you eat?" He answered her, "Because I said to Naboth the Jezreelite, 'Sell me your vineyard; or if you prefer, I will give you another vineyard in its place.' But he said, 'I will not give you my vineyard." Jezebel, his wife said, "Is this how you act as king over Israel? Get up and eat! Cheer up. I'll get you the vineyard of Naboth the Jezreelite."

So she wrote letters in Ahab's name, placed his seal on them, and sent them to the elders and nobles who lived in Naboth's city with him. In those letters she wrote:

"Proclaim a day of fasting and seat Naboth in a prominent place among the people. But seat two scoundrels opposite him and have them testify that he has cursed both God and the king. Then take him out and stone him to death.

So the elders and nobles who lived in Naboth's city did as Jezebel directed in the letters she had written to them. They proclaimed a fast and seated Naboth in a prominent place among the people. Then two scoundrels came and sat opposite him and brought charges against Naboth before the people, saying, "Naboth has cursed both God and the king." So they took him outside the city and stoned him to death. Then they sent word to Jezebel; "Naboth has been stoned and is dead." As soon as Jezebel heard that Naboth had been stoned to death, she said to Ahab, "Get up and take possession of the vineyard of Naboth the Jezreelite that he refused to sell you. He is no longer alive, but dead." When Ahab heard that Naboth was dead, he got up and went down to take possession of Naboth's vineyard. 1 Kings 21:5-16 NIV

Women are so influential. Ahab by himself would not have thought of killing Naboth for his piece of land. Dear wife, does your counsel empower your husband to do the wrong thing? Does your support deaden his conscience? Are you so ambitious that you have turned covetous? Do you count yourself a powerful woman because you can sacrifice morality for power?

2. Jezebel killed the Lord's prophet.

Now the famine was severe in Samaria, and Ahab had summoned Obadiah, who was in charge of his palace. (Obadiah was a devout believer in the Lord. While Jezebel was killing off the Lord's prophets, Obadiah had taken a hundred prophets and hidden them in two caves, fifty in each, and had supplied them with food and water.) 1 Kings 18:2-5 NIV

Jezebel was so mean that the same Elijah who prayed fire down from heaven and prayed for rain to cease for 3years didn't want to encounter her.

So, Jezebel sent a messenger to Elijah to say, "May the gods deal with me, be it ever so severely, if by this time tomorrow I do not make your life like that of one of them." Elijah was afraid and ran for his life. When he came to Beersheba in Judah, he left his servant there, 1 Kings 19:1-4 NIV.

THE JUDGEMENT OF JEZEBEL

"And also concerning Jezebel the Lord says: 'Dogs will devour Jezebel by the wall of Jezreel.'

*"Dogs will eat those belonging to Ahab who die in the city, and the birds of the air will feed on those who die in the country." (**There was never a man like Ahab, who sold himself to do evil in the eyes of the Lord, urged on by Jezebel his wife.** He behaved in the vilest manner by going after idols, like the Amorites the Lord drove out before Israel.)* 1 Kings 21:23-26 NIV

Jezebel signifies idolatry, shamelessness, wickedness, sin, greed, godlessness and immorality. Jezebel is not just the woman Jezebel; Jezebel is a spirit that characterises falsehood and wantonness. We know this because of the preceding paragraph. Thousands of years later, our Lord Jesus is still warning us against her.

Nevertheless, I have this against you: You tolerate that woman Jezebel, who calls herself a prophetess. By her teaching she misleads my servants into sexual immorality and the eating of food sacrificed to idols. I have given her time to repent of her immorality, but she is unwilling. So I will cast her on a bed of suffering, and I will make those who commit adultery with her suffer intensely, unless they repent of her ways. Rev 2:20-22 NIV

Tho MESSAGE Bible puts it this way,

"But why do you let that Jezebel who calls herself a prophet mislead my dear servants into Cross-denying, self indulging religion? I gave her a chance to change her ways, but she has no intention of giving up a career in the god-business. I'm about to lay her low,

along with her partners, as they play their sex-and-religion games. Rev
2:20-22

Jezebel's end was terrible. The end of all evildoers is
everlasting damnation. So, let's flee from sin and every
appearance of evil.

> *"This is what the Lord, the God of Israel, says: 'I anoint you
> king over the Lord's people Israel. You are to destroy the house
> of Ahab your master, and I will avenge the blood of my servants
> the prophets and the blood of all the Lord's servants shed by
> Jezebel. The whole house of Ahab will perish. I will cut off from
> Ahab every last male in Israel — slave or free. I will make the
> house of Ahab like the house of Jeroboam son of Nebat and like
> the house of Baasha son of Ahijah. As for Jezebel, dogs will
> devour her on the plot of ground at Jezreel, and no one will bury
> her." Then he opened the door and ran.* 2 Kings 9:6-10 NIV

And that was how Jehu was given the responsibility to pass
judgement on the house of Ahab; Jezebel, his wife and sons. Jehu thus
killed king Joram, Ahab and Jezebel's son.

> *When the lookout standing on the tower in Jezreel saw Jehu's
> troops approaching, he called out, "I see some troops coming."*
>
> *"Get a horseman," Joram ordered. "Send him to meet them
> and ask, 'Do you come in peace?'"*
>
> *The horseman rode off to meet Jehu and said, "This is what
> the king says: 'Do you come in peace?'"*
>
> *"What do you have to do with peace?" Jehu replied. "Fall in
> behind me."*
>
> *The lookout reported, "The messenger has reached them, but
> he isn't coming back." So the king sent out a second horseman.*

When he came to them he said, "This is what the king says: 'Do you come in peace?"

Jehu replied, "What do you have to do with peace? Fall in behind me." The lookout reported, "He has reached them, but he isn't coming back either. The driving is like that of Jehu son of Nimshi — he drives like a madman." 2 Kings 9:17-20 NIV

Quick! Get my chariot ready!" King Joram commanded.

Then King Joram of Israel and King Ahaziah of Judah rode out in their chariots to meet Jehu. They met him at the plot of land that had belonged to Naboth of Jezreel. King Joram demanded, "Do you come in peace, Jehu?"

Jehu replied, "How can there be peace as long as the idolatry and witchcraft of your mother, Jezebel, are all around us?" Then King Joram turned the horses around and fled, shouting to King Ahaziah, "Treason, Ahaziah!" But Jehu drew his bow and shot Joram between the shoulders. The arrow pierced his heart, and he sank down dead in his chariot.

Jehu said to Bidkar, his officer, "Throw him into the plot of land that belonged to Naboth of Jezreel. Do you remember when you and I were riding along behind his father, Ahab? The Lord pronounced this message against him: 'I solemnly swear that I will repay him here on this plot of land, says the Lord, for the murder of Naboth and his sons that I saw yesterday.' So throw him out on Naboth's property, just as the Lord said" 2 Kings 9:21-26 NLT

While some people are born into generational blessings because of the good deeds of their parents, king Joram inherited a death sentence because of his parents' blood-stained hands.

"And when Jehu was come to Jezreel, Jezebel heard of it; and she painted her face, and tired her head, and looked out at a window." 2 Kings 9:30 (KJV)

Then, as Jehu entered at the gate, she said," Is it peace, Zimri, murderer of your master?" And he looked up at the window, and said, "Who is on my side? Who?" So two or three eunuchs looked out at him. Then he said, "Throw her down." So they threw her down, and some of her blood spattered on the wall and on the horses, and he trampled her underfoot. And when he had gone in, he ate and drank. Then he said, "Go now, see to this accursed woman, and bury her, for she was a king's daughter." So they went to bury her, but they found no more of her than the skull and the feet and the palms of her hands. Therefore they came back and told him. And he said, "This is the word of the Lord, which He spoke by His servant Elijah the Tishbite, saying,' On the plot of ground at Jezreel dogs shall eat the flesh of Jezebel; and the corpse of Jezebel shall be as refuse on the surface of the field, in the plot at Jezreel, so that they shall not say, "Here lies Jezebel." 2 Kings 9:31-37

In 2Kings9:30, we saw why some people think applying makeup is synonymous with being a "Jezebel"; worldly and corrupt. Jezebel applied makeup so some think any woman who applies makeup is working in the spirit of Jezebel.

Identifying the spirit of Jezebel should centre around actions and not looks. Curbing the manifestation of the spirit of Jezebel would be more effective when we rebuke wickedness, expose falsehood and practice godliness. Focusing on make-up seems insignificant because one doesn't need to apply make-up to sin. I have met several sober, bland, no make-up-faced women whose deeds perfectly match Jezebel's.

The folks who think like this forget to note that Jezebel tied/adorned her head too. If we say using make-up is a sin because Jezebel applied makeup, then we should say tying of the head is a sin too. A decent appearance is great. I do not think using make-up is synonymous with being immoral, but I suggest using it in moderation instead of garishly. So, look good, but remember to pay more attention to your spiritual life—Who you are on the inside, what you think about, and, what motivates you are more important. So, remain kind, God-fearing and love-driven.

Do not let your adorning be external—the braiding of hair, the wearing of gold, or the putting on of clothing— but let your adorning be the hidden person of the heart with the imperishable beauty of a gentle and quiet spirit, which in God's sight is very precious. 1 Peter 3:3-5 *ESV*

Herodias

For Herod had arrested and imprisoned John as a favour to his wife Herodias (the former wife of Herod's brother Philip). John had been telling Herod, "It is against God's law for you to marry her." Herod wanted to kill John, but he was afraid of a riot, because all the people believed John was a prophet. Matt 14:3-5

Herod was the one who had ordered the arrest of John, put him in chains, and sent him to prison at the nagging of Herodias, his brother Philip's wife. For John had provoked Herod by naming his relationship with Herodias "adultery." Herodias, smoldering with hate, wanted to kill him, but didn't dare because Herod was in awe of John. Convinced that he was a holy man, he gave him special treatment. Whenever he listened to him he was miserable with guilt — and yet he couldn't stay away. Something in John kept pulling him back.

But a portentous day arrived when Herod threw a birthday party, inviting all the brass and bluebloods in Galilee. Herodias's daughter entered the banquet hall and danced for the guests. She dazzled Herod and the guests. The king said to the girl, "Ask me anything. I'll give you anything you want." Carried away, he kept on, "I swear, I'll split my kingdom with you if you say so!" She went back to her mother and said, "What should I ask for?"

"Ask for the head of John the Baptizer."

Excited, she ran back to the king and said, "I want the head of John the Baptizer served up on a platter. And I want it now!" That sobered the king up fast. But unwilling to lose face with his guests, he caved in and let her have her wish. The king sent the executioner off to the prison with orders to bring back John's head. He went, cut off John's head, brought it back on a platter, and presented it to the girl, who gave it to her mother. Mark 6:17-29 MESSAGE

Herodias was a model of Jezebel; adultery, hatred and murder were the order of her life. She was not afraid to kill John, and she didn't hesitate to use her young daughter, teaching her it was okay to ask for a just man's head. Even Herod was afraid to do something so dastardly.

Herodias shows us again the strength of a woman's influence. Whereas Eve's account points to the power of a wife over her husband, Herodias' story shows the power of a mother over her children. When children relate with their mothers, they do it with absolute trust. Virtually every child believes their mother is a saint, regardless of whether she is. Some kids lose unquestioning loyalty and hero worship as they grow older, but some do not. And, it is not necessarily because their mother is worthy of that adoration by being a good person; it is because they have been indoctrinated to see her as a perfect standard. Hence, they cannot tell when she does right from wrong.

Just like males, among the female folks, there are excellent women and evil women; some are born with these traits, but some learned to be evil because their primary influence was evil. They didn't stand a chance.

What kind of person would Herodias' daughter most likely turn up to be?

I can't say it enough. Women should be respected for their sheer influence. Respecting that influence is the easiest way to harness it beneficially. It will birth opportunities for training, transformation, participation and development that will positively impact generations.

Women are effortlessly, naturally powerful. Oh, if only all women were models of virtue! How beautiful it will be! Talk about positive impact - raising a generation of people who fear God, love others, hate sin and understand the sanctity of human lives.

The Wailing Women

This is what the Lord Almighty says: "Consider now! Call for the wailing women to come; send for the most skilful of them. Let them come quickly and wail over us till our eyes overflow with tears and water streams from our eyelids. The sound of wailing is heard from Zion: 'How ruined we are! How great is our shame! We must leave our land because our houses are in ruins." Jer 9:17-20 NIV

You women who are so complacent, rise up and listen to me; you daughters who feel secure, hear what I have to say! In little more than a year, you who feel secure will tremble; the grape harvest will fail, and the harvest of fruit will not come. Tremble, you complacent women; shudder, you daughters who feel secure! Strip off your clothes, put sackcloth around your waists. Beat your breasts for the pleasant fields, for the fruitful vines and for the land of my people, a land overgrown with thorns and briers — yes, mourn for all houses of merriment and for this city of revelry. The fortress will be abandoned, the noisy city deserted; citadel and watchtower will become a wasteland forever, the delight of donkeys, a pasture for flocks, till the Spirit is poured upon us from on high, and the desert becomes a fertile field, and the fertile field seems like a forest. Justice will dwell in the desert and righteousness live in the fertile field.

The fruit of righteousness will be peace; the effect of righteousness will be quietness and confidence forever. My people will live in peaceful dwelling places, in secure homes, in undisturbed places of rest. Though hail flattens the forest and the city is leveled completely, how blessed you will be, sowing your seed by every stream, and letting your cattle and donkeys range free. Isa 32:9-20 NIV

The above scripture is a call to be responsible. Some people think that being a good, god-fearing and submissive woman means being a door-mat. They erroneously believe that women should not take part in society. I wonder why anyone would think so, seeing that women are the most affected whenever things go wrong in society. Women should be as involved in policy making as men. Women should cry out against evil and stand for righteousness and justice. Women should intercede in prayer because God will hear and respond speedily.

To the indulgent, complacent, indolent women, arise, and start paying attention to what is happening around you; in your marriage, children's life, family, country, etc. We have to take our place before it is too late. Get on our knees, tender our petitions before God and keep at it till He intervenes. The heartfelt prayer of mothers and wives has delivered many destinies from the hands of the enemy into the power of GOD.

Take your stand, indolent women! Listen to me! Indulgent, indolent women, listen closely to what I have to say. In just a little over a year from now, you'll be shaken out of your lazy lives. The grape harvest will fail, and there'll be no fruit on the trees. Oh tremble, you indolent women.

Get serious, you pampered dolls! Strip down and discard your silk fineries. Put on funeral clothes. Shed honest tears for the lost harvest, the failed vintage. Weep for my people's gardens and farms that grow nothing but thistles and thornbushes. The royal palace is deserted, tthe bustling city quiet as a morgue, The emptied parks and playgrounds taken over by wild animals, delighted with their new home.

Yes, weep and grieve until the Spirit is poured down on us from above And the badlands desert grows crops and the fertile fields become forests. Justice will move into the badlands desert. Right will build a home in the fertile field. And where there's right, there'll be Peace and the progeny of Right: quiet lives and endless trust.

My people will live in a peaceful neighbourhood — in safe houses, in quiet gardens. The forest of your pride will be clear-cut, the city showing off your power leveled. But you will enjoy a blessed life, planting well-watered fields and gardens, with your farm animals grazing freely. Isa 32:9-20 MESSAGE

Dear woman, cry out against hate and restrain evil. Do not shy away from policy-making. Always lend your voice to right a wrong. Do not shy away from protecting others. Do not shy away from self-development. God expects you to be a blessing. Turn to Him in turbulent times. Trust Him as He leads you.

Learn to ask God to intervene. When women pray for repentance and mercy, things change. Women can birth a renaissance in the place of prayer. Do you know, dear woman, that prayer is a culture? A way of life? The more you pray, the more you like to pray. Interceding for our family, ministry, and city is our responsibility. Do not shy away from being an agent of positive change. Learn to pray until you glow, literally and practically. Pray without ceasing, whenever you feel the prompting, regardless of whether you have a prayer point, pray! Give thanks if you don't know what to say. A woman shared how The Holy Spirit prompted her to call, hold and declare specific words over her daughter after their routine evening devotion. After the prayers, they went to their respective rooms. A few minutes later, the little girl walked into her parents' room and said something stung her close to her left eye and on her arm. She said the sting seemed chilling and painful. Her mother, on noticing the swelling and pinkness in her arm and beside her eye, immediately followed her to her room. "Perhaps there was a tiny insect on the bed", she thought. As she looked under the duvet, she saw the last thing she was expecting. She shrieked in surprise and called her husband. "Honey, there is a scorpion on the bed". They did not know how the scorpion got there. They don't even live on the ground floor. After taking out the scorpion, and as they prayed for their daughter, the Holy Spirit reminded the mother of the special prayers she prayed earlier. The little girl held her mother and said, "It's no longer painful, I am perfect". They went to the hospital, and the doctor said the pain comes after 2hours. 2hours came and went with no need for pain relievers or antivenoms. 24 hours, 2000hrs, 200000 hrs, etc hours later and the pain never came, neither did any other symptoms. We have a God who answers prayers. We just have to learn to always pray. Hallelujah! Jesus Christ is the Lord.

Times of fellowship cannot be substituted or delegated. No one can have fellowship on your behalf. Ignoring personal times of fellowship and expecting the results of other people's relationship with God to make up is as futile as expecting to get nourished from a meal someone else ate.

Let the Holy Spirit who is your Comforter, Strengthener, Counsellor, Extraordinary Strategist, Advocate, Helper, Teacher, Intercessor and Standby do His work in you... Times of refreshing will come from His presence, it can only happen when you present yourself... Sometimes you just got to kneel there in worship for as long as necessary, long uncountable hours basking in His love and getting direction.

There are two phases of fellowship.

Seclusion and Inclusion. If you do one without the other, you will stunt your spiritual growth.

Seclusion: this is when you create a specific time and place for God. You only focus on God during this time; everything else is on hold while you worship, intercede, praise and pray. Practicing seclusion helps you grow fast and maintain a disciplined routine. It encourages deep meditation, assignments are birthed, and without distractions, the voice of God is heard more clearly.

Inclusion: This means having your prayer time while you go about your daily activities. Inclusion helps you pray all the time and get guidance on a real time basis. You pray while running your errands, doing chores; cooking, driving, etc.

Observing both cannot be overemphasised. Christianity is all about having a relationship with God through Jesus Christ. Having fellowship is the only way your relationship with Jesus gets continually strengthened. That is the only path to Christian maturity.

Practice to sit, do nothing, but sing praises to God and read his word. Be still, meditate, kneel or stand and worship God. Also, practice dwelling on God's presence as you drive, work, shop, etc.

The Wife of Pontius Pilate

While he was sitting on the judgment seat, <u>his wife sent to him,</u> <u>saying, "Have nothing to do with that just Man, for I have suffered</u> <u>many things today in a dream because of Him."</u> But the chief priests and elders persuaded the multitudes that they should ask for Barabbas and destroy Jesus. The governor answered and said to them, "Which of the two do you want me to release to you?"

They said,"Barabbas!" Pilate said to them, "What then shall I do with Jesus who is called Christ?" They all said to him, "Let Him be crucified!" Then the governor said, "Why, what evil has He done?" But they cried out all the more, saying, "Let Him be crucified!" When Pilate saw that he could not prevail at all, but rather that a tumult was rising, he took water and washed his hands before the multitude, saying, "I am innocent of the blood of this just Person. You see to it." And all the people answered and said, "His blood be on us and on our children." Matt 27:19-25

The blessing of being a discerning wife can preserve your family. Pilate could free himself from shedding the blood of an innocent man because his wife had a premonition. Women are very sensitive; this means they can pick signals from the realm of the spirit. Especially when they fear the Lord. And are prayerful and obedient to God. I must advise, don't use this ability to manipulate and deceive your husband or others. Do not be delusional or say the Lord has spoken when He has not. Things of the spirit are like two-edged swords. If you abuse the guiding principles, it will backfire and the joke will be on you, not others. Blessed is the woman who waits upon the Lord and speaks as He commands. Blessed is the man who listens to the wise counsel of a good wife, he will save himself from many follies.

The Woman With The Flow Of Blood

Now a certain woman had a flow of blood for twelve years, and had suffered many things from many physicians. She had spent all that she had and was no better, but rather grew worse. When she heard about Jesus, she came behind Him in the crowd and touched His garment. For she said, "If only I may touch His clothes, I shall be made well." Immediately the fountain of her blood was dried up, and she felt in her body that she was healed of the affliction.

*And Jesus, immediately knowing in Himself that power had gone out of Him, turned around in the crowd and said, "Who touched My clothes?" But His disciples said to Him, "You see the multitude thronging You, and You say, 'Who touched Me?'" And He looked around to see her who had done this thing. But the woman, fearing and trembling, knowing what had happened to her, came and fell down before Him and told Him the whole truth. And He said to her, "Daughter, your faith has made you well. **Go in peace, and be healed of your affliction.**"* Mark 5:25-34

Lessons

Even if medical science fails, God will not fail: The bible says that she had seen many physicians, suffered many things and spent a lot of money. But when she met Jesus, the story changed because the limitations of medicine do not apply to divinity. I have seen miracles and divine interventions. I have heard of healings that left doctors dumbfounded. The secret lies in the fact that Jesus is the same yesterday, today and forever. He healed the sick then, and He heals the sick now.

Faith in the power of God creates miracles: She said to herself, "if I touch the hem of his garment, I would be healed". What great faith…. what audacity! No wonder Jesus told her that her faith made her well. How profound. She believed so much in His power that she didn't need to be seen or touched by Him before getting healed. Our Lord Jesus said that if we have faith as tiny as a mustard seed, we can ask a mountain to move and it would. Do you believe in the power of God? Yes, you do?... Act on it. The woman did; she was acting on her faith when she came out in that condition- and then touched Jesus Christ despite the crowd thronging Him.

Jesus Christ loves you, and He wants you to be healthy and happy: Did you notice the Lord's response when she testified? He said, "go in peace, and be healed of your affliction". He didn't mind that she didn't seek His permission before placing a demand on His power. Jesus Christ is so compassionate. If you know nothing else about Christ, know this; He loves and cares about you deeply. It is so comforting to know that we follow and serve the Lord, who is moved by compassion.

But when He saw the multitudes, He was moved with <u>compassion</u> for them, because they were weary and scattered, like sheep having no shepherd. Matt 9:36

And when Jesus went out He saw a great multitude; and He was moved with <u>compassion</u> for them, and healed their sick. Matt 14:14-15

"I have <u>compassion</u> on the multitude, because they have now continued with Me three days and have nothing to eat. And I do not want to send them away hungry, lest they faint on the way. Matt 15:32

They said to Him, "Lord, that our eyes may be opened." So Jesus had <u>compassion</u> and touched their eyes. And immediately their eyes received sight, and they followed Him. Matt 20:33-34

Testifying: Another lesson here is that at the prompting of Jesus, she testified. Never be ashamed to testify to the goodness of God. Has God been good to you? Has He healed you and blessed you? Please say it because if the woman with the blood flow didn't share her testimony, we won't have known such a miracle happened. But because she did, several others have dared to believe in God too.

The Ten Virgins

"Then shall the kingdom of heaven be likened unto ten virgins, which took their lamps, and went forth to meet the bridegroom. And five of them were wise, and five were foolish. They that were foolish took their lamps, and took no oil with them: But the wise took oil in their vessels with their lamps. While the bridegroom tarried, they all slumbered and slept. And at midnight there was a cry made, Behold, the bridegroom cometh; go ye out to meet him. Then all those virgins arose, and trimmed their lamps. And the foolish said unto the wise, Give us of your oil; for our lamps are gone out. But the wise answered, saying, Not so; lest there be not enough for us and you: but go ye rather to them that sell, and buy for yourselves. And while they went to buy, the bridegroom came; and they that were ready went in with him to the marriage: and the door was shut. Afterward came also the other virgins, saying, Lord, Lord, open to us. But he answered and said, Verily I say unto you, I know you not." Matt 25:1-12

The wise virgins were the prepared ones. They knew that the coming of their Lord was not in their control; they couldn't influence the time, so, it was best to be prepared.

Preparation is the action or process of getting ready for an occurrence or opportunity.

Are you ready for life? If an opportunity comes knocking to help you achieve those goals, dreams and aspirations in your heart, will you be prepared? Preparation could mean taking classes, networking, etc.

Are you ready for eternity? Severally, the Holy Scriptures admonish us to live ready; our Lord Jesus shared many parables concerning this. Are you ready for the Lord's coming? Eternity should always ring in our consciousness because just as everything without God is nothing, anything without continuity is baseless. Life is vanity if all on earth is all there is. Apostle Paul said it is misery if our hope is only in this present world. A world plagued by so much uncertainty surely cannot be all.

Live life to the full. Make the best of every situation, but also live prepared. Even if you slumber, take extra oil so that when the time comes, you won't be found wanting. Rather, you can trim your lamp like the wise virgins and move on. Our Lord Jesus said, "Occupy till I come." Thus, you do not need to live apprehensively, rather, take charge in the name of the Lord, be happy and help others be happy too. Taking extra oil means ensuring your spiritual life is on point even as you navigate through the demands and vagaries of the physical world. Create time to maintain fellowship with God. Pray, study to know and do God's Word.

Like the five wise virgins, only share what you can. Avoid doing things that are detrimental to you and others. Someone said her organisation gave her a financial target for a good cause, but to achieve it, she had to prostitute with many men. I said she did the opposite of what the wise virgins did; she was giving out her oil to save others, but in the end, they won't be saved and she won't be saved too. So, in helping others, you do not have to self-destruct.

What shall it profit a man if he gains the entire world; wealth, accolades from men, numerous awards, etc, and loses his soul? The unwise virgins probably felt they were adequately prepared, but they weren't. Anyone can make such mistakes, especially if they lose sight of what is required and what is at stake. In chapter 13 of my book, THIS FASCINATING LIFE: Clarity is the New Gold, I wrote about delusions of safety. It is a very enlightening and empowering book.

In conclusion, one thing is certain; every woman is unique. After studying the lives of over 60 women, we see that no two stories are exactly alike. We also noticed that there were attitudes, habits and characters that God endorsed. Thus, let us replicate the beautiful traits and expunge the bad ones. I pray in the name of our Lord Jesus Christ that our hearts will always be yielded to the leading of the Holy Spirit... May we serve the only true God without reproach. May the teachings of our Lord Jesus Christ be our guide. May His Grace, love and power be expressed in and through us. May we prosper in good health and enjoy the loving-kindness of God. May we be true, humble and just. May we be lights in a dark world. May we be blessed and be a blessing to others. May we love righteousness and goodness. May our lives continually bring glory to God. May we always be happy. May we be prepared and worthy when the Lord shall come. May we be full of love always, because love never fails. Hallelujah.

Printed in Great Britain
by Amazon

76345886R00173